The
Tape-Recorded
Interview

EDWARD D. IVES

THE TAPE-RECORDED INTERVIEW

A Manual for Field Workers
in Folklore and Oral History

THE UNIVERSITY OF TENNESSEE PRESS : KNOXVILLE

Clothbound editions of University of Tennessee Press books are printed on
paper designed for an effective life of at least 300 years, and binding
materials are chosen for strength and durability.

Library of Congress Cataloging in Publication Data

Ives, Edward D.
   The tape-recorded interview.

   Edition for 1974 published under title: A manual for
field workers.
   Bibliogrpahy: p.
   Includes index.
   1. Folk-lore—Field work. 2. Oral history.
3. Magnetic recorders and recording. 4. Folk-lore—
Theory, methods, etc. 1. Title.
GR45.5.193 1980   390'.072.   79-20527
ISBN 0-87049-257-8
ISBN 0-87049-291-8 pbk.

"Some things can be done as well as others"   —SAM PATCH

Contents

ILLUSTRATIONS

Acknowledgments

Many people have contributed in one way or another to producing this manual, and while a detailed listing of their individual contributions might acknowledge my debts to them more adequately, I hope they will accept the simple listing of their names as at least a token of my gratitude, which is real: Bob Bethke, Gordon Bok, Joan Brooks, Jan Brunvand, John Burrison, George Carey, Mike Chaney, Gould Colman, Jim Denton, Linda Edgerly, Lisa Feldman, Bill Ferris, Lydia Fish, Carl Fleischhauer, Henry Glassie, Joe Hickerson, Louis Iglehart, Flo Ireland, Ernest Kennedy, Waldo Libbey, Fred Liebermann, Dick Lunt, Roger Mitchell, Lyn Montell, Monica Morrison, Gerry Parsons, Sandy Paton, Chuck Perdue, Neil Rosenberg, Dick Tallman, Barre Toelken, Dale Treleven, Ken Whitney, Wig and the gang at *Foxfire,* and D.K. Wilgus. Cheryl Lavertu and Gerri Moriarty typed the final manuscript and, along with Joan Brooks, helped with the proofreading. Finally, it is entirely appropriate for me at this time to acknowledge a long-standing debt to Dick Dorson, the youngest of the grand old men.

Preface

In June of 1973, *Foxfire*'s Eliot Wigginton asked me to give a lecture on "Collecting and Archiving" to a workshop composed of high school students and their faculty advisers from all over the country (not to mention Haiti and Jamaica) who were interested in beginning Foxfire-type projects of their own. Later, Ann Vick and Brian Beun of IDEAS, co-sponsor of the workshop, asked me to amplify my remarks for publication in their newsletter, *Exchange,* which went out to all such projects around the country.

The more I worked on it, the more I saw how much I needed such a guide for my own classes. The result was "A Manual for Field Workers," which I produced in a very simple mimeographed form. In no time at all, I was getting letters from folklorists, oral history types, and prospective foxfirers, inquiring about its availability or asking for a dozen copies, and soon the modest edition was exhausted. However, inquiries continued to come in, and it was therefore decided to issue a slightly augmented form of the manual as volume XV of *Northeast Folklore* (1974).

I say "slightly augmented," because while the mimeographed form served my own classroom purposes well enough, I now wondered about "broadening" it substantially, in order to make it more generally applicable. Correspondence with several people whose opinions I respected reinforced my own hunch that the manual would probably lose as much as it would gain by becoming much more generalized. Therefore, with the exception of some small changes and additions (such as material on the use of photographs in interviewing), this second edition of the manual remained very little changed from the first, local in focus and specialized to the procedures of the Northeast Archives of Folklore and Oral History. The problems it addressed, though, were much the same problems that field workers anywhere would have to face.

Evidently, many people found our solutions and attempts at solutions helpful because this new version of the manual sold out in less than two years. Meanwhile I had begun to make some needed additions and corrections based on our continued experience here at the Northeast Archives. The most notable addition was an essay on the tape recorder, since I had found that most field workers—especially (but not exclusively) novice field workers—had little or no idea of how one worked or what they could reasonably expect from it. At this point, we at the Northeast Folklore Society were about to consider a new edition, when the University of Tennessee Press asked to do the present volume.

This time around, however, it was decided not to tie the manual quite so specifically to the Northeast Archives but rather to present material that any archives could fit into its program after adding a few mimeographed pages detailing its own particular procedures. Even so, I have continued to use the Northeast Archives as my chief example, just as I have used my own field experiences more than those of others, and for the same simple and excellent reason: that is what I know best.

There are two themes running through this book that deserve advance comment. The first is a rather dreary one: my insistence on good bookkeeping techniques at every step—keeping copies of letters, checking and rechecking equipment, maintaining a journal, making complete opening and closing announcements, numbering tapes systematically, keeping track of which picture goes with which interview, cataloguing, transcribing, and the like. None of this is much fun, and all of it may seem peripheral to the real business of interviewing, but it is part of the craft, just as hours of French polishing is part of the guitar-maker's craft. Show me someone who "hasn't time for all that fussing," and you will have shown me someone who really should be doing something else.

My second emphasis is not at all dreary: the common man. People coming to this manual from history, especially from oral history, have often spoken of it as "non-elitist." No question about it, the common man *is* the Northeast Archives' emphasis, just as it is mine personally. Most of our work has been devoted to documenting the lives of common men and women—woodsmen, river-drivers, fishermen, farmers—and I happen to consider *Let Us Now Praise Famous Men* the sixty-seventh book of the Bible. But that emphasis should in no important way make this book less useful to anyone engaged in "elitist" studies. Elitism/nonelitism is a ridicu-

lous polarity to begin with. Between the two there is no great gulf
fixed. No man is common and great men are a dime a dozen, and
getting cheaper.

The research method discussed in the following pages involves
two separate but interrelated activities. First, it involves going out
into the field for extended, tape-recorded interviews with people
about some aspect of their experience on which you wish to gather
information. Second, it involves processing the tape produced so
that its contents will be easily available not only to you but to others
who wish to use it in their own research or to check the accuracy of
yours. At the very least, that means identifying and documenting
the tape systematically, cataloging and indexing it, and placing it in
an archives. It also means that at some point the tape will need to be
transcribed, either completely or in part. Obviously, this method is
not a short-cut to anything. It is painstaking, time-consuming, and
expensive work and involves several steps, all equally important.
The actual interview, the hour or so spent with the informant, may
be the most exciting and dramatic step, but any interview that is not
well prepared for or that is not carried out with full regard for the
fact that others will be making use of it is going to waste a lot of
people's time.

The first decision to be made is whether such a method suits your
purposes. It may be that you'll do better just taking some notes
which you can expand on later, or you may decide that even a note-
book is too obtrusive. For example, a student of mine, interested in
how her fellow students used proverbs on a day-to-day basis, spent
her time simply listening carefully. Later she wrote down what
proverbs she had heard, noting where, when, and under what circumstances (by whom, to whom, in connection with what) they
were used. The present method would have been useless to her, and
any attempt to adapt it would have been an incredible waste of time.
Another student wanted to find out how well known a particular
legend was in a certain town. He simply went to that town, posing as
just what he was (a curious tourist) and started talking to people he
met. In a short time he brought together about a dozen versions of
the legend by jotting each one down as soon as possible after he
heard it. Had he begun by going around with a tape recorder and

jamming a mike in people's faces, he probably would have achieved very little except to make a spectacle of himself.

Some people may wish to use the tape recorder simply as an interim note-taker. They will listen to the tape later on, take final notes on what is relevant to their needs, and then either use the tape over again or stick it in the back of a drawer for possible future reference. They will have no intention of placing the tapes in an archives, which means that clarity of the signal or proper documentation are minimal considerations for them. Such users may still find some of the following pages useful.

The present method is not a panacea; it is one way of working amid many. But if you decide that the extended taped interview that has been carefully prepared for, documented, and placed in an archives is the way you want to go, then all of what follows will be relevant, and you can start down the road.

The
Tape-Recorded
Interview

1. How a Tape Recorder Works

You will not be traveling this road alone. You will have a constant companion, your tape recorder, and you must learn to be at ease with it and to know what it can and cannot be expected to do. To be sure, many people who take pictures don't know anything more about a camera than that you put the film in here and look through there and push this button, but no one who calls himself a *photographer* can afford that kind of ignorance. On that analogy, no one who uses a tape recorder as a tool of his trade (as both folklorists and oral historians do) should be allowed to indulge in the dubious luxury of saying, "I don't know much about these gadgets." What follows in this chapter will not make you an expert, but it might keep your constant companion from becoming your nemesis.

We will be talking, here, about tape recorders in general, not any specific machine. You will have to find out how the discussion applies in detail to any machine you may be using, but that will not be a problem. I have tried to avoid technical terms as much as possible, and I am sure I have frequently committed the sin of over-explaining. Yet everything in this chapter grew out of my responses to multitudinous questions, all the way from "How d'ya turn it on?" to "What's that hiss?" Let no one feel insulted by my seeming to belabor the obvious. Each item here was far from obvious to someone.

A tape-recording system has three basic components: the microphone, the recorder itself, and the tape. The microphone transforms sound into a varying electric current, which is then fed into the recorder, where it activates an electromagnet (the "head"). This head then magnetizes a coating of iron oxide on a constantly moving ribbon (the tape), imprinting on it a pattern (you can't see it, but it's very much there) that varies as the sound varies—a "loud" sound will make a stronger imprint than a "soft" one, a "high" pitch will make a different pattern than a "low" one, and so on. Then when you want to play the recording back, you pass this magnetized tape over another magnet, the "playback head." This time the process is reversed: the magnetized tape activates the head, creating an electric current of varying strengths which drives a "speaker," creating sound. Since the imprinted magnetic pattern is not destroyed by playing the tape, you can listen to a recording over and over again. When you erase a tape, you "scramble" or "randomize" the magnetic patterns, and you can then use that tape over again. It's as simple as that, if you don't press for too many details.

Cassette versus Reel-to-Reel

Probably the most immediately apparent distinction between different kinds of tape recorders is in the method of supplying the tape. With reel-to-reel machines, you put a full reel on one side, thread the tape past the heads, and attach it to a take-up reel on the other side. With a cassette machine both the supply and the take-up reels are enclosed in a plastic case, which you simply snap into place, automatically putting the tape in position to move past the heads. From the standpoint of how a tape recorder works, there is very little difference between the two; the cassette is simply a specialized kind of reel-to-reel operation. Therefore all the following explanations will be in terms of reel-to-reel machines, with special qualifications given where necessary for cassette operations.

But there *are* differences between the two. The cassette is obviously simpler to load: snap it in and you are ready to go. On the other hand, threading a reel-to-reel machine is not a particularly demanding task—certainly no more of a problem than putting a roll of film in a camera. But if something goes wrong inside the cassette, say the tape breaks or becomes tangled, then the convenient package becomes a first-rate nuisance. It is true that splicing kits are available for cassettes, but it is still one hundred percent easier to splice a reel-to-reel tape, if it breaks or gets tangled. At present writing, it is still possible to get a better signal (that is, a better quality sound) on a reel-to-reel than on a cassette tape, but cassettes are improving all the time, and besides, for general interview purposes the difference in quality is not that important, especially if you use the very highest quality cassettes available.

The biggest problem with cassette tape is that it is a poor medium for preservation. For long-time archival storage—an important consideration—the best advice I can give is that open-reel tape is still by far the best. Therefore, even if your field recordings are made on cassettes, you or your archives should make provision for transfer to open-reel tape as soon as possible. This is a bit of a nuisance, but provided that you have the transfer equipment, it is hardly a compelling reason for not using cassettes in the field.

The more compelling arguments against cassette recording have less to do with the cassettes themselves than with the inflexibility of most recorders designed for them. Cassette machines have almost completely taken over the low-to-medium cost (say less than $300) home recorder line, and every attempt has been made to simplify their operation. First, all of them—even the expensive ones—operate at one speed only (1 7/8 i.p.s.), which is perfectly adequate for speech but really not adequate for music, since your basic rule is the higher the tape speed the greater the fidelity. Reel-to-reel machines offer a choice of speeds, allowing you to match the speed to the task, a decided advantage.

Second, and this is a far more serious matter in my opinion, most cassette machines do not allow you to control the recording level yourself. It is entirely automatic, the machine responding to the loudest sound it hears. We will have more to say about this "automatic level control" later on, but for now let me only say that if you have to buy a cassette recorder—and the way the market is going that is a real possibility—make sure it has the option of manual level control (sometimes called "manual over-ride") in addition to the standard automatic.

To sum up, then, if you use first-line cassettes, if you make sure your machine has the manual level control option, if you are modest in what recording quality you expect (especially in the recording of music), and if you can transfer your recording to open-reel tape for storage, then you should have no great problem with cassettes. I still recommend reel-to-reel, but that preference is not something I will either argue about or insist on any more. Besides, in terms of what is available in the stores today, that preference may be just a bit academic, unless you are prepared to spend several hundred dollars for your machine.

How About Stereo?

In principle, stereo is simply two synchronized tape recorders whose
mikes are some distance apart laying down separate signals on the
same tape, which, when played back through separate speakers,
gives an effect of "roundness," of two ears listening, as it were.
Good stereo equipment gives wonderful results, but it is expensive.
If one is recording an orchestra, I will say unhesitatingly it gives better results, but in the kind of one-to-one recording most of us do
most of the time in folklore and oral history, I don't see that it of-
fers any advantage at all. I will have more to say about stereo later
on, but my advice is that you would do better to get the best mono-
phonic machine you can afford, rather than putting money into
stereo.[1]

Power Supply

Obviously, in order to run a tape recorder you have to have electricity, and this is supplied by either house current or batteries. Many
machines today run on both (that is to say, either), but since the
ground rules are a little different for each, we'll take them up sepa-
rately. House current (110 volt, alternating current, 60 cycles) has
the advantage of being essentially constant, but notice that I said *essentially* constant. That is, it doesn't run down the way batteries
can, but it does vary by as much as 10 percent—occasionally even
more than that. For reasons we need not go into here, these fluctua-
tions are much more common in rural than in urban areas, and while
most machines have built-in "capacitors" to compensate for these
"surges," they *can* cause noticeable variations in tape speed. All I
can say is that in twenty years of field recording I have never been
bothered by surges, but since other field workers tell me they have
been, I mention them here as something you might want to inquire
about in the area where you plan to work.

1. For an interesting adaptation of stereo equipment to recording what is going
on in something like a dance, where the music is recorded on one channel while on
the other channel the field worker describes what people are doing, see the two articles by Ivan Polunin listed in the Bibliography.

Another disadvantage of house current, again one that seems to occur most frequently in rural areas, is that occasionally your recording will pick up a "hum" from it. I have never had this problem myself, but it has been reported to me by others more than once. If you do use house current and notice a hum you cannot otherwise explain, you may be able to eliminate it by reversing the plug in the wall socket. That failing, try switching to batteries for subsequent recordings.

But perhaps the biggest disadvantage of depending on house current is that it tethers you to available electrical outlets; that is, you have to take their location into account when you decide where you are going to hold the interview. In modern houses that isn't apt to be a problem, but in older ones—especially those built before the days of electricity—you may discover that there is only one base socket in the room where you are going to hold the interview, and that is already overloaded by the television set and two lamps. For this reason, I always make an extension cord part of my standard equipment when I set out to interview someone new. And by the way, the power cord is usually a separate accessory for most small machines, not something permanently attached, and it is very easy to overlook in the rush of preparing for the interview.

It is probably clear by now that I recommend using batteries whenever possible. You don't have to worry about the location of outlets, and you don't have to unplug your informant's TV to set up your tape recorder. The greatest advantage is that you can move around freely. I remember one time when a man wanted to show me where an old sawmill had been; I was able to continue the interview as we drove along in the car and as we walked among the remains of the old mill itself. Battery operation is convenient and flexible, no doubt about it, but like all flexible conveniences it has its own set of problems.

The big problem with batteries is that they have a nasty tendency to run down, which is to say they lose power with use, causing the tape to run more slowly than it should (this leads to the "chipmunk" effect when you play the tape back later at proper speed). Many tape recorders automatically adjust for this power loss, but you can count on that adjustment only up to a certain point. I have never known a machine that would not slow down when the batteries became weak. Now all battery-operated machines have visual battery-strength indicators built into them, which is a big help; sometimes, however, batteries will be fine at the beginning of an interview but fade without your knowing it as the interview progresses. Even if you train yourself (as you should) to check the indicator several times during the interview, the discovery that the batteries have faded leaves you with the dilemma of proceeding and making the best of the situation, or putting in a new set of batteries or switching over to house current in the middle of an interview. The chance of battery failure is about ten times that of a "power surge," and for this reason alone I used to recommend the use of house current whenever possible. But I finally discovered that for some three years I had not followed my own advice, with absolutely no resultant battery problems.

The difficulty, of course, is not with the batteries but with the operator. Batteries will serve you well, so long as you know what you can expect them to deliver *and then stay well within the limits of those expectations.* Sometimes the manufacturer of the battery will publish life-expectancy figures (occasionally right on the battery), but almost always the directions for the tape recorder will contain such information. Play it safe: read these suggestions as maximum expectations.

There are two basic principles that should never be forgotten when you are using batteries. First, they are meant for intermittent, occasional use (an hour or two at a time), not for extended power supply. Second, they will recuperate when not in service. It will be best, then, to use them for a short period, then put them aside for a considerably longer period. Of course recuperation is never complete, and the older a set of batteries gets, the less you should expect from it. Keep careful track of how many hours you have used a set; there is no substitute for the confidence that knowledge can give you.

Batteries vary in type and quality, both affecting how long they last and how well they recuperate. As a rule, the more they cost, the longer they last, but there are several main types you are apt to run into. Carbon-zinc or "flashlight" batteries are sold everywhere, and they are by far the cheapest batteries you can get. In no way can I recommend them. They will serve in a pinch for most work in our line, so long as you only use them for an hour or so each day and then give them overnight to recuperate before using them again. But never count on them for more than about three hours total use. For about half again as much money you can get "heavy-duty" carbon-zinc batteries, and I would trust them for about half again as long. In either case, never leave c-z batteries in your machine for any length of time (like weeks), because they are damnably apt to leak. At the least that makes a mess; at the worst it can cause expensive damage.

Alkaline (manganese dioxide) batteries cost about four times as much as standard flashlight batteries, and they last about four times as long. You can also count on them for longer periods of service, and they require less time to recuperate. In addition, they hold up better when not in use, being less apt to leak (although I would not leave *any* battery in a machine for long, idle stretches).

Mercury batteries are less generally available than either the carbon-zinc or alkaline types. They last about ten times as long as flashlight batteries, perform even better for long periods, and are proportionately more expensive. Their chief advantages, beyond longer operating life, are that they do not fade and they have almost unlimited shelf life, an important advantage if there will be long stretches (like months) between your field trips. However, not all machines will accept mercury batteries. They will "fit" well enough, but some brands have reversed polarity, which means they will send the current through the machine the wrong way and damage the circuitry.

Nickel-cadmium batteries are sometimes called "rechargeable." They are rather heavy, very expensive, and not usable in all machines. However, if you are in a situation where you have to use your machine for long periods every day, and if you can remember to recharge them afterward for just the right amount of time (like overnight), one set of these batteries can be used dozens of times over, which in the long run will bring their cost down below even the cost of the cheapest flashlight batteries.

To sum up all the information on power supply, I suggest using alkaline batteries, but I also recommend you never go into the field without the power cord, which will allow you to use house current in an emergency. There are many variables, of course (like how long the batteries have been on the dealer's shelf and how tough your particular machine is on batteries), but you can trust a set of alkalines for about sixteen hours, and I wouldn't hesitate to use them for a two-hour session (especially early in their life) or to use them more than once on the same day. Finally, always follow religiously the manufacturer's recommendations on how to recharge batteries or whether to attempt to recharge them at all.

One basic rule will help you get the most out of any batteries: *Never use them for anything but interviews.* Use house current for everything else: cataloging, playback, even fast-forward and rewind if possible (both of which use an astonishing amount of power). With almost all tape recorders, you need not remove the batteries when you change power sources; the house current bypasses them completely, thereby allowing your batteries to recuperate for the next interview.

The Controls

Just about every tape recorder will have the following controls, but their location and arrangement will vary tremendously. They all do the same things, but you should learn where they are on your machine —and how to use them.

On/off switch.   Many machines do not have a separate on/off switch. On most of the inexpensive cassette machines, putting the machine in one of its modes (i.e. play, record, fast forward, or rewind) turns it on, while taking it out of mode turns it off. Then too, on many machines there is a second on/off switch on the side of the microphone (this sometimes causes confusion: see the section on "Immediate Action" below).

Volume.   On some machines, the same knob controls the volume for both recording and playback; on others there are separate controls for each of these. By the way, for our purposes you can accept the terms "gain," "volume," and "level" as roughly equivalent. If someone suggests that you "cut your gain" or "check your level," you should make some adjustments in the volume. On many machines there is a system called *automatic level control* in which you do not set the recording volume: it sets itself. If the sound to be recorded gets weaker, the a.l.c. ups the gain; if the sound gets louder, the a.l.c. lowers the gain, and it constantly adjusts the gain to the strength of the sound. It is altogether ingenious and convenient, the greatest thing since the automatic choke, but like that automotive convenience it has limitations and even creates some problems of its own.

In the first place, a.l.c. should never be used to record music, because it will completely muddle whatever dynamic relationships (louds and softs) there may be in the performance. Second, you should remember that it always adjusts the gain to the loudest sound available. If that sound happens to be the informant's voice, fine, but a.l.c. is extremely sensitive to background noises (for some reason it seems especially to favor television and radio sound—even from the other room!). Then too, the ambient noise will swell up to fill any silences that last over a couple of seconds (remember that a.l.c. is constantly looking for a sound to record, regardless of whether it happens to be a voice or a washing machine). When the voice comes in again, it takes a.l.c. a split second to adjust, but that may be enough time to cause you to lose the first word or so in an answer to a question. Besides, I find this swelling up of ambient noise into silences in the interview can be extremely annoying.

If you have to conduct an interview in a noisy place, say an office with typewriters clacketing and people talking, the best advice I can offer is to use manual level control, keeping the gain as low as possible and the mike as close to the informant's mouth as you can conveniently have it. Of course, if your machine has *only* a.l.c.—and that's all that most inexpensive cassette machines have nowadays—you're out of luck. Automatic level control is satisfactory for some purposes, but I would consider it a minimum standard for our line of work that a machine have manual control too. If it came to a choice, I would opt for manual control every time. The convenience of a.l.c., like the convenience of cassette loading, has been grossly exaggerated. It only takes a little while to learn how to set your own level, and at least half the time you will get better results that way than with a.l.c. Almost never will you get worse.

Tone. This control adjusts the amount of "bass" or "treble" in the signal. Turning it clockwise (right) usually enhances the treble quality, counterclockwise (left) the bass, while right in the middle is sometimes spoken of as "flat." On most machines, the tone control only works for playback; the setting has no effect when you are recording. But on some machines it works on "record" as well. With the latter kind of equipment, you will have to experiment to find what setting will give you the best quality recording signal. The manufacturer will probably have some suggestions in the "directions," but let me add one warning of my own. In the world of cheap electronics (and that is where most of us live) "bass worship" is rampant. Do not equate a good signal with prominent bass, especially since in our line of work we emphasize clarity, not richness. You may get a better signal by emphasizing the treble slightly, or even turning it up all the way.

Play.   Pressing this control starts the tape moving by the head, and if there's a signal on the tape, you'll hear it played back. Sometimes the control is marked "play," sometimes "forward" (or even "fwd"), and sometimes simply with an arrow pointing to the right. That is all we need to say about it for now.

Record.   Frequently, though not always, the record button is red, to distinguish it clearly from the others. Get this button pushed and you are making a recording, if you have the mike plugged in (otherwise all you will do is erase whatever happens to be on the tape). I say "get it pushed," because this button almost always has to be pushed in conjunction with some other button: the "play" button, the pause control, or a special safety button. This "tie in" or "interlock" feature is supposed to remind us of what we are about to do and thereby prevent accidental erasures. It's a very effective feature, and you'll be glad for it, believe me.

Pause.   This control simply stops the forward motion of the tape without taking the machine out of mode (it stays in "record" or "play"). Sometimes it is an entirely manual control, in which case releasing it starts the tape again; sometimes you move it in one direction to pause, the other to start again. In all forms, it is a handy gimmick, but if yours is the kind that does not release when you take your finger off it, you'd better recognize that fact and remember to do whatever you have to do to release it. Forget this, and you will wind up with no recording at all.

Fast Forward. This mode is sometimes called "advance," and sometimes it is marked with double arrows pointing to the right. Its function is to move the tape ahead in a hurry. If, for instance, you have already recorded on the first third of the tape, and you want to begin your present recording after that, "fast forward" will carry you ahead in seconds to where you wish to begin, when it might take several minutes to move ahead in "play."

Rewind. Sometimes called "reverse," sometimes "review," and sometimes marked with an arrow or a double arrow pointing left, this mode is simply "fast-backwards," moving the tape to the left swiftly. Let it run on, of course, and this mode will put all the tape back on the left-hand (i.e. "supply") reel.

Stop. No matter what mode you happen to be in, push this button and you will be out of it. Frequently this control operates with a loud "click," even a substantial "clack," leaving you no doubt that the machine has stopped. No further explanation is necessary, excepting to say you should be clear on the distinction between "stop" and "pause," but I do have one suggestion. Always switch from one mode to another (e.g. "play" to "fast-forward") *by moving through "stop."* That is, if you are recording and you want to rewind, push "stop" first, then "rewind." Manufacturers almost universally suggest that this procedure saves wear and tear on the switches. It also helps avoid putting excess strain on the tape.

Monitor. This control is usually on one side of the machine, or even on the back. When the monitor is turned on, you can hear what is being recorded played back through the speaker (or through a headset, if you have one plugged in). If you turn it off, the speaker is disconnected while you are in "record." It is not something you are going to use much, if at all, in our line of work, but you should know about it because of "feedback." For example, say you are recording, and you notice that the level is too low, so you turn up the gain to get more volume. Suddenly the tape recorder starts howling —and that is just the word for it! What's happening is that your tape recorder is acting as a little public address system. You speak into the mike, and the sound coming out of the speaker is loud enough for the mike to pick it up again, whereupon it feeds this signal back into the machine, whereupon it comes out of the speaker again, and so forth, until it is amplified into a screech. That is feedback. It sounds frightful, but you can kill it by simply turning the monitor switch to "off" or (on the UHER) by pulling out the "volume" knob, disconnecting the speaker.

Sometimes there is a "music/speech" switch, usually on the mike but occasionally on the chassis. The label is reasonably self-explanatory, but I will say this: I've occasionally neglected to push the lever into the "music" position when recording someone singing, and I haven't noticed any excruciating difference in recording quality. The appropriate setting might make a significant difference in recording a string quartet, though. On the other hand, you do get a little sharper, crisper signal if you record interviews with the switch in the "speech" position. Leave it there, as a rule.

Indicators

Position indicator.   This device, sometimes called the "index" or "digital counter," can help you locate material on a tape, and you will have to use it when you make your catalog. Always set it to zero at the very beginning of the *tape* (not the beginning of the *interview*) when you are cataloging. It is of no particular use when you are recording, except that it can tell you where you left off and where to begin again if you remembered to set it at 000 when you started. There are two points of potential confusion, though. First, the indicator does not measure feet, inches, or any other standard units of length. It is simply a *counter.* Second, counter numbers worked out on one brand of machine are not necessarily valid for any other brand. In fact, you can assume they will *not* be. There will even be some variation from machine to machine within one model! But counter numbers established on one machine *can* give you a pretty good *relative* idea of where to find something, even on another machine. They are extremely useful, that is, but don't expect too much of them.

Level indicator.   The level indicator is a device that you can look at to find out how well you have adjusted the gain to match the incoming sound signal in order to get the best recording level. On most recorders now it is a meter (commonly called a "VU meter"), a needle that moves up and down a scale on which the left-hand two-thirds is white and the right-hand third red. If you have the gain too low, or if the incoming signal is too weak to record, the needle will remain at rest at the left of the scale. If you have the gain too high, or if the incoming signal is too strong, the needle will spend most of its time over in the red or (in extreme cases) be "pinned" all the way to the right. The trick in getting a good level is to adjust gain to signal so that the needle moves up to the red but not into it, except in occasional moments of sudden loudness (someone who has been talking quietly suddenly shouts at the dog). I will have more to say about level later on.

Battery strength indicator.   This is almost always displayed as part of the VU meter, but it has its own scale. Usually there is a special button to activate it, and if the needle goes up into the designated "safe" area (and the further up it goes into this area the better), your batteries are probably all right.

The Tape Transport System

In order for the "heads" either to imprint a signal on the tape or play back a signal already imprinted, there must be a mechanism to move a supply of tape by the head at a precisely determined and constantly maintained speed. That is the job of the tape transport system, which usually consists of the following visible parts (of course there will be a motor or motors and a series of belts and gears to run the whole works, but the only thing you need to know about them is that they are inside). We will move from left to right.

The supply reel.   This is the full reel of tape on the left spindle. The spindle usually has three little wings on it that fit into corresponding slots in the reel. Never force a reel onto the spindle; if it doesn't drop right down into position, just rotate it lightly until the slots and wings line up, and it will fall into place. Many machines also have a locking device on the spindle so that you can use the machine in any position and the reels will not fall off. When the tape is advancing, the supply reel is not powered, or is powered just sufficiently to prevent it from creating any kind of drag. On "rewind" the motor delivers its main power to this reel.

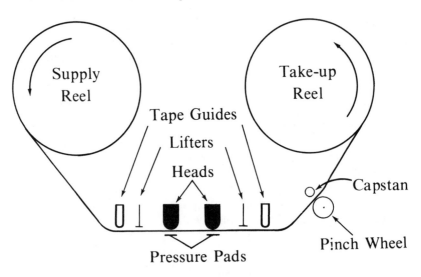

Figure 1. Tape Transport System

Tape guides. These guides are variously placed and variously constructed. They may be plainly visible, or they may be under the cover that protects the heads. Whatever the arrangement, they will be on both sides of the heads, and their task is to keep the tape precisely positioned as it goes by them.

Pressure pads. These little pads are mounted on a pressure generating device that pushes the tape up against the heads in both "record" and "play" modes. You can see how this device works by watching the heads carefully and at the same time pushing the "play" button slowly. Not all machines use the pressure pad system of keeping the tape in contact with the heads. In fact, most of the more expensive and sophisticated machines do not, but the system is common in the "one motor" budget machines most of us use most of the time.

Lifters. On some machines (not all by any means), when you activate "stop," "fast-forward," or "reverse," a little post moves out between the heads (sometimes there are two—one on either side of the heads) and lifts the tape away from them, thus saving both heads and tape from wear and tear through abrasion. The only problem they present is that you sometimes get the tape hooked on them when loading the machine. Recognizing the presence of lifters on a given machine will, of course, help you to avoid the problem.

Capstan and pinch wheel. This is the heart of the whole transport system. It is always to the right of the heads and is more than likely under the same cover that serves to protect them. The tape passes between the bright metal capstan and the rubber pinch wheel (or pressure roller), and in either play or record mode the pinch wheel holds the tape tightly against the capstan. It is the powerful little revolving capstan that keeps the tape moving at exactly the right speed.

Automatic cut-off. Not all tape recorders have this gimmick, but most do. It is a spring-operated device over or through which the tape passes, and when the tape runs out on one of the reels the spring flips and turns off the machine. All it does is prevent the tape from flapping a lot once it is all on one reel. I have always considered this a dubious advantage, but the device may be there, and if you have threaded the tape through it incorrectly your machine will not operate. So look for it.

Take-up reel. This is the right-hand reel that picks up the tape paid out by the capstan as it comes off the supply reel. It does not pull the tape through the machine; the capstan does that. In fact, during "play" and "record" the take-up reel turns just fast enough to collect the tape passed on by the capstan. On the other hand, during "fast-forward," the full power of the motor is delivered to the take-up reel, and then it *does* pull the tape through.

Loading the Tape Recorder

Loading the machine in preparation for recording involves attaching a full supply reel and an empty take-up reel and properly threading the tape between the two. To begin, you simply put the full reel of tape on the supply spindle, making sure that it seats itself securely, then seat an empty reel *of the same size* on the take-up spindle. If your machine has devices to lock the reels in place, make sure you engage them at this time. Also make sure the machine is in the "stop" mode, so that there is a clear passage between the pressure pads and the heads, between the capstan and the pinch wheel, and through or over the automatic cut-off. Then pull a length of tape off the supply reel and drop it down through the above-mentioned "clear passage." Since the manufacturer often leaves very little clear passage at best, this maneuver can be a little tricky. On some machines, for example, the tape has an exasperating habit of riding up over the heads or, as I mentioned, of getting hooked on the lifters.

Assuming that you have the tape threaded properly, with the coated side toward the head and capstan, the backing side toward the pressure pads and pinch wheel, you are now ready to attach the tape to the core of the take-up reel. On some reels there are special slots you can slip the end of the tape into, or you can learn to make special little loops with the tape, but I always prefer simply to lay the end flat on the core and to rotate the reel a few times. The tape binds on itself and holds quite snugly. It doesn't matter how you secure the tape. Just check and make sure the coated side is toward the core and the backing side is out.

Of course if you are using cassettes, all you do is snap one into place. As Figure 2 should make clear, the capstan sticks up through a hole in the cassette. When you put the machine in either play or record mode, the pinch wheel closes on the capstan just as it does in a reel-to-reel machine, but the heads move up against the tape rather than vice-versa. Otherwise, the principles of operation are identical.

Tape Speed

I have already pointed out that, for a recording to be of any use at all, the tape must be kept moving by the head at an absolutely con-

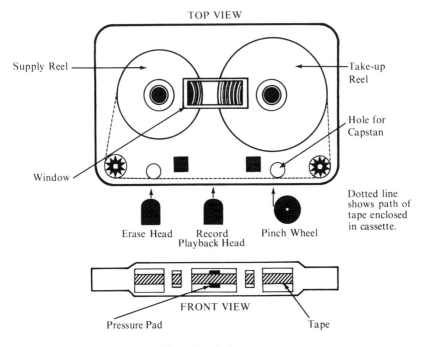

Figure 2. A Cassette

stant speed, and it must be played back at exactly the same speed. Any speeding up or slowing down during either record or playback will cause distortion. For now, however, we will assume that everything is working fine. At what speed should you set your machine?

We are caught in a double stretch here. The faster the tape moves, the higher the quality of the recording; the slower it goes, the more we lose this or that nuance of the sound we wish to record. On the other hand, the faster it moves the less recording time we have before we have to change reels, and the bigger our tape bills become. Fortunately, not every recording situation requires the high fidelity fast tape speeds can deliver. The question is, How fast is fast enough? Fortunately too, the industry has agreed to limit us to five standard speeds (measured in inches per second or "i.p.s."): 15, $7\frac{1}{2}$, $3\frac{3}{4}$, $1\frac{7}{8}$, and $\frac{15}{16}$. Most machines, however, have only the mid-

dle three speeds. (For present purposes, we will talk in terms of a 5"
reel of "standard" 1½ mil tape—that's 600 feet).

At 7½ i.p.s., a 600 foot tape will run through in fifteen minutes.
That's not much time, but if you are recording music, especially in-
strumental music, it might be advisable to use this speed. At 3¾
i.p.s., the same 600 foot tape will run through in half an hour. You
can do a reasonably good job of recording vocal or even instrumen-
tal music at this speed. At 1⅞ i.p.s., this tape will last an hour, and
the quality is absolutely all you need for any interview situation.
Since most interviews tend to run about an hour or less, this has always seemed to me the optimum speed for our work. (Note: Cassette machines have *only* this speed, which, as I have already said, is
one of the things I dislike about them.) If you have to record music
at this speed, you can, but I would never set about to use it for this
purpose. At ¹⁵⁄₁₆ i.p.s., you can run the same tape for two hours
without changing, and the reproduction quality is reasonable for interview purposes. However, since most transcribing equipment will
not handle this slow a speed, such a recording will be difficult to
work from later on. Besides, there seems to be little gained from the
extra recording time, considering the length of the average interview.

It should be clear, then, that 1⅞ i.p.s. is perfectly adequate for almost any interview situation, considering a mix of reproduction
quality, available time, and compatibility with transcribing equipment. If, however, singing, fiddling, or other musical performance
is going to bulk large in the interview—and this is something that
you know ahead of time—3¾ i.p.s. would be a better choice. If you
know that you will be recording music, and if it is doubtful that you
could ever get back with better equipment, play it safe and use 7½.
One final bit of advice: *do not change speeds in the middle of an interview,* and never shift back and forth. If you are recording some
music at 3¾ and your informant then decides to tell you his life
story, leave the speed at 3¾. It will cost a little more in tape, but it
will save a lot of confusion later on.

The Heads

There are three kinds of heads: the erase head, the recording head,
and the playback head. On most machines (all but the very expen-

sive ones, in fact) the record and playback heads are one and the same. In record mode the head *prints* an image on the tape; in playback mode it *responds* to the image already printed on the tape. This dual function allows us to talk about three heads, even though we see only two.

The erase head is located on the left, which means that the tape passes over it before it gets to the record/playback head. In playback, the erase head does nothing at all, but in record mode it completely scrambles any pattern that has already been printed on the tape, thereby giving the record head a blank tape to work on. It is always best, though, to begin recording with a clean tape, either one that has been bulk-erased ahead of time or (better yet) a brand new tape, because occasionally the erase head on a machine will not do as clean a job as it should. Still, if you have to use an unerased tape, it should serve well enough.

The record head is the one on the right, and as was indicated at the outset of this chapter, it is simply a sensitive and responsive electromagnet. It imprints a variety of magnetic patterns on the tape, in response to the varying intensity of the electrical charge, corresponding to the quality and intensity of the sound picked up by the mike.

Schematically, the relationship of the heads to the tape in record mode looks like this:

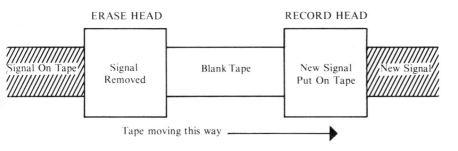

Figure 3. The Relationship of the Erase and Record Heads

That is really all you need to know about the heads, excepting for two things that can go wrong. First of all, the heads are apt to get dirty after a while, not only from ordinary dust but also from a certain amount of the iron oxide coating from the tape rubbing off on them. Since a clear recording requires that the tape be in direct contact with the head, a coating of dirt will not help anything. Clean the heads every once in a while, say after every ten or twenty hours of use. A Q-tip dipped in isopropyl alcohol will do the job nicely, but don't bear down too hard. (Scratch the heads and you will be worse off than before!) You should also clean the tape guides and the capstan in the same way at the same time. And go easy with the alcohol; you don't really need much.

Second, an electromagnet is only a magnet when a charge of electricity is flowing through it. No charge, no magnetism, therefore (in the case of a recording head) no imprint on the tape. But after an electromagnet has been subjected to electrical charges over and over for an extended time, it tends to develop a little residual magnetism, which is to say it becomes a continual magnet, however weak. Now a head with residual magnetism will print something on the tape even when it is not supposed to, and the residual magnetism will also fuzz and distort every signal coming in. Therefore, every once in a great while, get the heads demagnetized, especially if you have been noticing some distortion. You can even learn to do it yourself, with a little gadget you can buy for the purpose.

Half-track, Stereo, and All That

A recording head will lay down a pattern only on that part of the tape with which it comes directly in contact. If the tape is a quarter of an inch wide (and it is), and if the head is the same width, obviously the head will imprint the full width of the tape. That is what is known as a full-track recording. Only the most sophisticated and expensive machines have this full-track capability. If the head is only an eighth of an inch wide and is set to move along the upper edge of the tape, it will only imprint that upper half, leaving the lower half blank. Then, when the entire tape has run off the supply reel onto the take-up reel, if you flip the take-up reel over and put it on the supply reel spindle (placing at the same time the empty supply reel on the take-up reel spindle) you now have what was the blank lower half in position to move by the head and receive a signal of its own. This is what is called a half-track recording, and it is what we find on almost all monaural machines. (Note: Actually the head is designed to imprint slightly less than half the tape width, enough less to leave a slight blank space down the middle). Schematically a half-track recording looks something like this (think of the reels as already having been "flipped"):

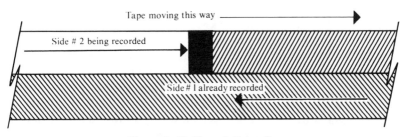

Figure 4. Half-track Recording

Theoretically, it is possible to put any number of tracks on a tape, but none of the machines you are apt to use in our line of work will have more than two, with the exception of machines with stereo capabilities. As I pointed out earlier, a stereo machine is simply two tape recorders, and each of them lays down a separate track on the tape through its own head. In order to allow for the economy of recording in both directions, most stereo recorders use a four-track system, two in each direction in the following pattern (again, think of the tape as having been "flipped" to begin recording on the second "side"):

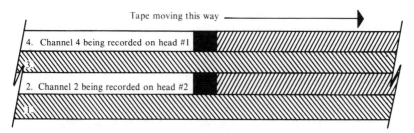

Figure 5. A Stereo Recording

Thus, tracks one and three are recorded in one direction, two and four in the other.

It should be clear now why you cannot play a stereo tape back on normal two-track mono equipment: the half-track head will pick up both tracks one and two (or three and four)—one playing forward, the other backward—at the same time. Conversely, if you try to play a full-recorded two-track monaural recording on stereo equipment, each head will pick up a different track, again one of them playing normally, the other backward. A fully-recorded stereo tape cannot be played back on two-track mono equipment. If you have to use a stereo machine in the field and if the archives with which you will be working cannot process stereo tapes, you can get by if you remember only to record on one channel each way. Only use head #1 or head #2, and use the same one in each direction. On the other hand, if for some reason you must play a two-track monaural tape back on stereo equipment, simply play it back through one channel only.

Tape

Recording tape is a plastic ribbon, and no matter what kind it is (or whether it is cassette or open-reel) it has three basic components: first, a backing, the physical "tape" itself; second, the coating of iron oxide on which the signal will be imprinted; and third, some sort of a bonding agent that holds the other two together. It used to be possible to speak of the coated side as "dull", the backing side as "shiny," and in a general way it still is, but some of the newer tapes have a polished oxide surface and a backing that is dulled purposely for contrast. At any rate, you should check to see which side is which on whatever tape you are using, remembering that the coated side must always come in contact with the heads.

The subject of coatings and bonds gets highly technical, and we need not go into it here. Any good quality tape today will have a coating that is more than adequate for all our purposes, and while bonds used to be a problem, they don't seem to be any more. Some surfaces are better than good, some are even better than that, and the prices increase proportionately. Stay away from bargain or nonstandard brands (or no brand at all, sometimes called "white box"). They may be great, they may not. In general, stay with good middle to first-line tapes (like 3M-176, for example). Even backing isn't much of a problem any more, but there are some things to watch out for. Keep in mind that the perfect backing is one that will last forever without getting brittle and will not break or stretch under normal or even abnormal conditions. Paper was the first backing material used, but it simply was not tough enough. Then acetate backing became the standard. It was non-stretching and about ten times stronger and longer-lasting than paper, but it would break and there were complaints that in time it tended to become brittle and go to pieces (I might say here that I have some acetate tapes that are twenty years old and still perfectly usable, but then . . .). Then mylar came along. It was great for long life and just about unbreakable, but it would stretch under even slightly excessive strain, as when the machine was stopped suddenly. (I have even heard people say it would stretch if left standing on the reel—like a nylon tire). Many of us stayed with acetate, preferring a tape that would break and could be repaired to one that would stretch and could not be. But today this problem is pretty well worked out; tensilized (a sort of pre-stretched) mylar or other polyester backings are just about ideal and are getting better all the time.

Tape comes in different weights, measured in thickness. The standard is 1.5 mils, "extended play" is 1.0 mil, and there is an even thinner tape only half a mil thick. The advantage of the thinner tape is that you can get more on the reel and therefore have to change tape less frequently. The disadvantages are that it is more prone to stretching and "print-through" (that is, once it is on the reel, one layer is apt to transfer its magnetic imprint to the layer directly beneath it), which gives a kind of echo effect on playback. I recommend that you use only standard 1.5 mil tape. Many people have told me they have had no problems with 1 mil tape, getting little or no print-through and finding the extra time advantageous. But half-mil tape is an invention of the Devil. If there is any way for it to get tangled or caught in the works, it will. Avoid it.

Having spoken of tape "getting caught in the works," I would like to temper my earlier enthusiasm for the new polyester tapes. There will come a time when something will go wrong; the tape will get a sudden yank and get jammed in the sides of the reel or wrapped around the spindle. Or the capstan will not stop completely and the tape will creep up under the cover; then when you start up again the tape will get a terrible jerk. Under any of these circumstances, acetate would break and you could fix it, but for all its advantages *polyester will stretch.* Nevertheless, if something untoward like this happens to you, listen to the damaged section, because it just may play back adequately (though it will look awful). If it doesn't, all you can do is cut out the stretched section and make a splice.

Splicing is a simple enough matter. Almost every tape box includes splicing directions on the inside of the cover. An edit block, a single-edged razor blade, and a roll of splicing tape should be standard equipment in the field; usually these can be bought in kit form at any store that sells tape, and once again these kits have full directions for use printed on the back. One comment, however: frequently tape-box directions recommend that you cut slightly into the tape when you make your final trim, but it is best to cut as straight as possible. In any splice, the adhesive is going to bleed out at the edges after a while, and the "gibson girl" type cut makes it just that much more likely that the adjacent layers of tape will stick together.

Everything I have said here about open-reel tape also applies to cassettes. "C-60" cassettes are the equivalent of standard 1.5 mil tape, "C-90" of 1 mil tape, and "C-120" of half-mil tape. There is one thing to watch, though. A C-60 cassette will run only thirty minutes before it has to be flipped, a C-90 forty-five minutes, a C-120 one hour, and the C-120 is just as subject to print-through and tangling as half-mil tape. If you are going to use cassettes, it is even more imperative than with open-reel tape that you use first-line quality; with the slow speed and extremely narrow track, everything depends on it. And by the way, for equivalent quality, inch for inch and minute for minute, cassettes turn out to be more expensive than open reels.

The Microphone

The "mike" is the device that changes the sound into electrical impulses, and this is not the place to get into a full-scale discussion of how it does that. We will just accept the fact that it does. I will also assume that you will use the mike that comes with the tape recorder, and there is no reason in our line of work why you shouldn't, because these little mikes are remarkably good. Still if it turns out that you will be recording a lot of music, or if you just want to improve the quality of your recordings generally, one of the first things you should consider (assuming your machine is a decent one to begin with) is getting a better mike. But once you decide to move in this direction, make sure you get good advice (and that probably means something better than the guy at the local music store), because not all machines will accept all mikes. There are things like impedance (high or low) that have to be matched carefully. That, however, is beyond our present purpose.

Some tape recorders have built-in mikes—right in the chassis— and some people say they have had good luck with them. I have always found them second-best to "external" or plug-in mikes, mainly because no matter how good they are they always seem to pick up some motor noise, which is annoying. If your machine has one of these built-in mikes, you will have to determine for yourself what its limits and capabilities are, but I recommend against their use if there is a choice—and there usually is a choice.

Some mikes are designed to pick up sounds only from a particular direction; you can even get one that you have to aim like a gun! But most of the mikes we deal with are of two basic kinds: omnidirectional or cardioid. The omnidirectional mike, as its name implies, is designed to pick up sounds from all directions equally, which means that if you put such a mike halfway between you and your informant, it would record your voices at about the same level (assuming your voices are equally strong). Most mikes, though, are made to favor sounds from directly in front of them; their sensitivity drops off as the sound source moves to the sides, and they are least sensitive to sounds from directly behind them. Plot this range on the floor and it comes out in a kind of heart shape, which is why it is called cardioid, with the apex in front, the "dent" directly behind the mike. Both omnidirectional and cardioid mikes have their advantages and disadvantages in interview situations, but it is at least good to know which kind you have. Usually the specifications in the book of instructions coming with your machine will give you this information, but if they don't you can establish it for yourself when you play "the game" described below.

Just where should you place the mike relative to the person you are interviewing? That is something that will vary from mike to mike and machine to machine, not to mention informant to informant. You should make sure that your voice comes through clearly too, although it need not be at the same level as the informant's. Keep this basic principle in mind: the clarity of your recording (and minimizing of extraneous noise) is almost entirely a function of how close you can get the mike to the informant's mouth and how low you can keep the gain while still getting a good signal. The further you have the mike from the informant and the higher you have to bring up the gain, the more "hollow" the voice will be and the more background noise you will get. But if you hold the mike right up to his face, or if you flip it back and forth the way you see television newsmen do, you will create a situation in which neither of you can relax much. You will have to compromise. Perhaps you can set the mike on the little table next to his chair, or even over the back of his chair (I have done that once or twice). Try some of these placements at home and see how they work. But remember the basic principle: Get the mike as close to your informant as you can without making it so obtrusive as to be a nuisance. On this matter of obtrusiveness, by the way, I would rather not talk *over* a mike, preferring always to place it left or right of the informant's and my line of sight.

This is probably as good a place as any to stress how very sensitive to extraneous noises a microphone can be. Let me give an example: you are interviewing an elderly man, and his wife says, "Well, I'll just leave you two alone," whereupon she goes into the kitchen and washes the dishes. You hear nothing at all during the interview itself, but later on when you play it back, the crash-bang of the crockery fair to drowns out the interview. Try as best you can to hold the interview in a place where there won't be a lot of background noise. If you think such noise will present a problem, try going ahead with the interview; then say, "Hold it a minute, I just want to see if this machine's working all right," and listen to a little of what you have recorded. If you have a problem, see what can be done about it without upsetting the entire household. But frankly, just being mindful of the possibility of problems of this type will eliminate about two-thirds of them.

"The Game"

In order to learn what your mike can or cannot do—in fact it is a good way to learn the strengths and weaknesses of your recording equipment in general—I recommend the following game. Set the machine up in such a way that you can see the VU meter from some distance away, which will probably mean setting the machine on its side (you may find it easier to enlist the aid of a friend to stand by the machine and tell you what the needle is doing at any particular moment). Put a tape in, set the machine in record mode, and talk, all the time telling yourself what it is you are doing and how the machine is responding at the moment. Something like this (I am assuming you have manual level control, but the game is useful for finding out what automatic level control can do, too):

> Now I've turned the thing on, and I'm talking in my normal voice directly in front of the mike and about two feet from it. The gain is set at 6 and the needle on the VU meter is moving up to but not into the red area. Now I'm moving back to about four feet from the mike and I haven't changed anything else, and the needle is only moving up about a quarter of the way, except when I SHOUT, when it jumps up almost to the red. O.K., now I'm moving over to the right to about forty-five degrees, still about four feet away, and the needle is hardly moving at all, just a little. Now I'm moving in to turn the machine some so I can see the meter from over here—I haven't moved the mike or changed anything else—and O.K. now I'm back out again at four feet, and the needle isn't moving at all now. Now I'm directly behind the mike, and the needle still isn't moving, even when I SHOUT—well, it did move just a little then, but. . . .

Keep this game up, trying different settings and distances, letting your voice be loud and soft, always telling yourself three things: where you are in relation to the mike, what the needle on the VU meter is doing, and what level you have set the gain at. (*Note*: On some machines the gain control is not calibrated, in which case you can use the analogy of a clock face: "I've set it at three o'clock," etc.) Try as many different combinations of control settings as are available to you. If your machine has a built-in mike, try that, and then right after it try the external mike. See whether the tone control is operative in record mode, and try comparing what you get when you move the music/speech switch from one to the other. Try turning on an electric fan or a television set in the background. If you have a cardioid mike, what happens when you aim it straight up? Don't hurry the game. Take plenty of time, and try everything.

One of the most important things you can learn from this game is how low a level you can record at and still get a decent signal. Start with the gain at zero and move up all the way to the top by steps, giving yourself enough tape to listen to at each step. When you play this section back, you may find that you get a perfectly good signal at ten o'clock, even though the needle was only moving a little. Since meters vary in sensitivity and get out of adjustment easily, you may find that you get a better recording at low level than when the needle is moving (as it ideally should for the best signal) just up to the red. You will certainly discover what a fuzzy signal you get when you over-record, when the needle stays in the red most of the time.

That brings me to a final—and by this time rather obvious—note on recording level: it is by far the lesser of two evils to under-record than over-record. With a weak signal you can usually turn the volume up on playback to compensate. At worst, there are laboratory ways of boosting a weak signal, but there is nothing that can be done to correct the distortion caused by over-recording. Of course, the dilemma is a false one, because with a little care, you can record at the proper level almost every time.

Immediate Action: When "It won't go."

It is bound to happen sometime, and you can almost count on its occurring just as you are ready to begin your interview: you turn the machine on and nothing happens. Your batteries are in good shape —everything was working fine when you left home this morning. You know your batteries are reasonably fresh, and you know you haven't accidentally left the recorder running since the last time you checked it (that *can* happen with some machines, like the UHER 4000 series, by the way). Now what?

It may be that something in the works *has* "blown" or "burned out," which will mean you are really out of business until you can get it fixed, but the odds are a good ten-to-one against it. Run through the following "immediate action" steps before you conclude that doomsday has come:

1. If there is an on/off switch on the side of the mike (sometimes called a "servo-" or "remote-control"), check to make sure it is in the "on" position. In my experience, this check has solved about one-half of the "won't go" problems.

2. If there is an automatic cut-off device, check to make sure you have threaded the tape through it properly. On most machines, it is all but impossible to get the tape through it incorrectly, but check it anyhow.

3. If you are using house current, check the plug on the recorder end. Wiggle it a little, and give it a good push to assure yourself that it is fully seated. Then do the same thing on the wall outlet end. Try flipping the plug over. If you are satisfied that the problem is not poor contact (and that the cord is not broken), it is just possible that the outlet is at fault. Try plugging a lamp into it (I mention this because there are two outlets in my summer study, neither of which is connected to anything!).

4. If you are using batteries, open the battery compartment and check to see that the batteries are installed properly. Are any of them in backwards? If not, then simply roll the batteries with your hand without removing them; sometimes just a tiny bit of corrosion will form and keep one battery from making complete contact with the next one, and rolling them will be enough to make that contact again. If that fails, simply take the batteries out and put them back in again in a different order. It sounds ridiculous, but it works. Failing that, forget the batteries and plug in to house current.

Some people recommend having a spare set of batteries around —a great idea, but in the fifteen years I have been using battery-powered machines I have never (a.) remembered to bring them or (b.) been inconvenienced by not having them. Others recommend bringing along a back-up tape recorder—another great idea, if you can afford it! Of course, these auxiliary or back-up systems become more necessary the further afield you go and the longer you plan to be away from home. But that is a matter of planning an expedition, not immediate action. For the average day-tripping involved in most of the work readers of this manual will be doing, the four steps I have suggested will make the difference between "no-go" and "go" ninety percent of the time.

If you have simply *read* this far, you already know more about a tape recorder than half the people out using them who say they are "collecting folklore" or "doing oral history." And now if you read carefully the directions that come with your particular machine, and if you will conscientiously play my suggested "game," you will be better prepared to get to work than seventy-five percent of them— and at least as well prepared as ninety percent of them. That should (in the original and etymological sense of a good old word) *encourage* you some.

2. Interviewing

Finding Informants

"How do you find these wonderful people?" That is a question I have often been asked, and it implies that "informants" are a special kind of animal and that finding them is something like catching night-crawlers: "you gotta be quick!" I often answer that question by saying that everybody is a potential informant for something, which is usually accepted as a polite evasion on my part. But my answer is an honest one, and the first thing that you have to do in this line of work is to stop looking for that wonderfully gnarled old woman sitting in front of her foxfire in a just-right-squeaking rocking chair and accept the possibility that your neighbor's teen-age son home on vacation from Groton may be a perfect informant. The important thing is to have a very clear idea what it is you want to find out. Once you know that, you will probably have very little trouble finding good people to talk to.

You can begin by "asking around." If, for instance, you have become interested in "Old Dalton," whose stories you can remember your father quoting with great amusement, your father, then, should be the first person you turn to as a possible informant: "Remember those stories you used to tell me about Old Dalton? Well, I'm . . ." Chances are he'll balk a bit—"Oh good Lord! You don't want *them*. Why they're nothing but a lot of lies anyhow!"—but if you persist and make it clear what you are doing, all will be well. One person will lead to another, usually: "Your Uncle Floyd knows a lot more of those stories than I do. Why don't you go see him?" Fine, go see Uncle Floyd, but only after you have made it clear to your father that you want the stories the way *he* remembers them too. Accept such references as new prospects, but never let this "handing on" become a "putting off." You will not only not find the pot of gold, you will probably lose the rainbow as well.[2]

2. This advice on "starting at home" should be balanced against what is said about "stranger value," in the section on *The Initial Contact*.

I have warned against searching for the perfect or ultimate informant, but that is not to say there won't be special people you should
see. You may know someone who is an exceptional storyteller or a
singer with a considerable local reputation. You should of course
see these people, but the point is that you should not spend all your
valuable time looking for or waiting on such an informant when the
stuff of folklore and local history is alive all around you.

One of the best methods I know is to publish a letter in whatever
newspaper it is that people in that area read, or write an article and
ask the editor if he will use it in a coming edition. In that letter be as
specific as you can about what it is you are looking for, while at the
same time being careful not to "lead" by giving the very information you hope to get. If you are looking for information on that
"notorious liar," I would advise against calling him "probably the
most famous story-teller in these parts," because it is possible there
are others far better known that by some cultural coincidence you
simply have not heard of. I also advise against saying you are
"writing a book." That phrase conjures up all sorts of sugar-plum
visions in people's heads, and it may discourage some from responding because they are convinced that they don't know enough
to be able to help you. Let it be known that you have heard of this
man and the stories he used to tell, that you will be visiting the area
soon, and that you would like to hear ("at the address given below")
from anyone who can tell you anything at all about the man or his
stories.

I have had great success with this simple ploy. In writing about
Larry Gorman and Joe Scott, since the "community" was actually
all of Maine and the Maritime Provinces of Canada, I published
such letters in practically every daily and weekly newspaper in the
area, and I received dozens of responses. In writing about Lawrence
Doyle, I only published a letter in the Charlottetown (P.E.I.) *Guar-
dian,* and here again I got excellent results. I even heard from many
people off the Island who told me that someone "back home" had
clipped my letter and sent it on to them.

Some of my best informants have come to me *via* the newspaper
letter, but not everyone who writes in is going to be a good informant, of course. Unfortunately, there are a lot of inveterate letter-
writers in the world, people who evidently write simply to write. But

don't take chances by sorting people out before meeting them; the only thing you can do is see them all. Some excellent informants sound impossible in their letters. It also happens that a lot of people will write you not because *they* know something but because they *know* someone who does (though this may not be clear in their letters). In other words, they are good secondary informants. And that leads me to mention another great advantage of the newspaper letter: it alerts many people who would not write themselves but who nevertheless will see the letter. Frequently, on the recommendation of a secondary informant, I have gone to see someone and had him say, "Oh yes, you're the fella that's interested in Lawrence Doyle. How are you making out?" That was said with genuine interest, and the person often adds that he did not write me because he did not feel that he had enough information or that everyone knew what he knew.

I have yet to find a situation where my letter to the newspaper has worked against me in any way. First of all, it has found me many good informants, both directly and indirectly. Second, it has allowed me to go into a strange area with some sort of identity. I have specific people to go see, and when I see them I have something specific to talk about. I may be a stranger, but there is nothing mysterious about me at all.

Two further bits of advice on newspaper letters will be helpful. Ask the paper to send you a dated clipping of your letter (include a stamped self-addressed envelope with your request). And promptly answer every letter that comes to you, keeping a carbon of your reply. In other words, keep good records. I would not mention this, except that I know from experience it is too easy *not* to do; and if you don't, you can be sure you will be sorry for it at some point.

And a final warning on informants: people will sometimes direct you to the local historian, saying that he or she "has a lot of that old stuff." Unfortunately, many local historians have little understanding of and even less interest in the kind of material you will be looking for. Many of them are still caught up in "great man/significant event" history and will not consider a local farmer who used to make up songs important enough for their attention. Nor will they be much help when it comes to folklore, much of which, as far as they are concerned, is simply "not true." Or they may be amateur collectors themselves, in which case you would only be collecting from another collector. But there are splendid exceptions, and such exceptions can be a tremendous help in suggesting people to see, things to check out, and the like.

The Initial Contact

Assuming, then, that you have become well-acquainted with your tape recorder, that you know what it is you want to find out, and that you have the names of people you want to see, your first job is to break the ice and make an appointment with your prospective informant. I have found it a good idea to write a letter first (see my sample letter in the Appendix); not only is it polite, it identifies you very well and gives the informant something to think about. If your work is being sponsored by some organization (say a college or an historical society) whose letterhead stationery you can use, it helps some by giving you a sort of instant respectability.

Once you have sent the letter, wait a few days and then follow up with either a phone call or a visit (or both) to make arrangements for the first interview. Don't call too soon; give the letter enough time to get there and the informant enough time to turn the whole idea over in his mind a bit. And don't wait too long; in either case you lose the real value of writing the letter. As a rule of thumb, let the letter arrive, then wait one or two days, but never wait more than a week.

Of course, a letter may be much more than is required. You may already know the informant, or the informant may contact you first (say in response to your newspaper letter), or a third party (say a son or a daughter) may encourage you just to call or drop in ("Mother's always home and I know she'd be delighted to talk to you"). Such arrangements are fine, and they probably will work out all right, but it never hurts to be a little circumspect in the face of such encouragement. If it sounds like a good lead, and if you are reasonably certain that the person making the reference knows what you are doing, you might ask that person to call on your behalf. Generally, I prefer to keep things in my own hands, though, by calling myself. And if time and circumstances permit, I write a letter.

Some people tell me they hesitate to write a formal letter because they "don't want to get the poor soul all worked up." I suppose it could work out that way, but I have never known it to. Others have said that if they write—or even call—the prospect has more of a chance to say no, while if they just drop in the battle is half won already. There may be special circumstances where the surprise attack is justified, but it *is* pushy, and I avoid it whenever I can (which is almost all the time!). Besides, you would normally write an opening letter to a retired general or actress you wished to talk to; why not offer the same courtesy to a laboring man or a farm wife?

Generally, then, a letter followed by a phone call is ideal. A letter alone is all right (and of course if there is no phone it is all you *can* do). A phone call alone may be all that is required, but think carefully about why you are not going to bother with a letter. Finally, try not to arrive on someone's doorstep unannounced in any way; it may be necessary, but it usually isn't.

There are two questions that students often ask at about this point. The first, and by far the more common, frequently comes out something like this: "Do you think it's going to make a difference that I'm a girl when I go talk to Mr. Bilodeau about lumbering?" My answer is usually, "Of course it's going to make a difference, but I can't tell you what kind of difference." I have seen it happen that a man who was reluctant to talk to a woman at first came very quickly to enjoy the whole thing thoroughly once he discovered that she knew what she (and, of course, he) was talking about. Sometimes a woman will open up to a male interviewer after she had been very careful and even shut-mouthed with a female. Just about every time I have predicted how the man/woman of it would work out in some particular case, I have been wrong, which means that I have stopped predicting. All I can suggest is that you be sensitive to this problem, but no one should ever be scared out of attempting an interview because of it. It is much more important that the informant have confidence that the interviewer knows what he or she is talking about, and a recent incident speaks to that point. Two girls had gone at different times to interview a man in connection with our work on Argyle Boom.[3] At a later time I went to see him myself.

3. Edward D. Ives, *Argyle Boom* (Orono, Maine: *Northeast Folklore* XVII (1976).

"I'm glad you're here," he said. "You know, it's kind of hard to explain these things to a girl." What he told me was just about the same as what he had told them, which they had understood thoroughly. In other words, the difference in interviewers had no effect on the success of the interview, even though he thought it did.

The second question is only a bit different from the first: "Wouldn't it be better if Edgar went to interview Mr. Bresnahan? I mean, that's his uncle, after all." The answer is, "Maybe, but not necessarily." The rationale behind the question is that Edgar won't have to go through the ice-breaking and will know better what to ask. The rationale behind the answer is that there is much Edgar won't ask, because he already knows all about it, and Mr. Bresnahan will not explain some things for the same reason. There is something called "stranger value," which means that none of these assumptions exist between people who don't know each other, and sometimes people will say things to strangers that they would feel awkward or silly saying to members of the family. It's kind of a paradox, but people frequently find that being interviewed by a close friend or relative is an odd and not entirely pleasant experience, while they will feel quite at ease with a stranger under the same circumstances. The paradox is less obvious if you are asking for specific items like stories or songs than if you are after more general cultural information, but it is still there. I would far prefer to interview a stranger, myself, but there are plenty of examples of successful interviewing of close relatives and friends.

When you make your appointment for the preliminary interview, be sure the time and place are clear to both of you. Do you need directions to reach the house? What time is convenient? May you bring a friend (if that is part of your plans)? If you can, send the informant a quick note confirming the time, place, and circumstances you have both agreed to. If there seemed to be any vagueness about the appointment ("Next Friday afternoon? Yeah, I'll probably be here all right"), you might want to call the day before and check for sure. If you still get a "probably," there is little to be done, because you can hardly insist. But that is simply a way of speaking some people have, and I can assure you the person "probably" *will* be there. Risk it. And if you are not sure of your directions, allow plenty of time for getting lost.

The Preliminary Interview

You have made your initial contact by phone, letter or both, and now here you are on the doorstep, about to meet your informant for the first time. I have always found this the most anxious moment of the whole game: the time when I actually come face-to-face with my prospective informant. I have practiced all kinds of self-deceptions so that I could put it off for an hour or a day ("I'm going into town for a cup of coffee first." . . . "Morning's a bad time." . . .), a point I would not bother to mention except that the novice may take some comfort in realizing that the so-called expert gets the same butterflies in his stomach for the same reason—and always will. But if you have made your initial contact by letter, phone, or both, you may also take comfort in knowing that the worst is already over, and you are not arriving a perfect stranger.

The preliminary interview is several things at once. It is, first of all, a time for you and your prospective informant to get acquainted, but it is also a time when you can answer questions and explain more fully what it is you are doing and decide whether or not this particular prospective informant is in fact a good informant. We will take up the last of these considerations in more detail.

There are two basic questions you can use as guides. First, *does this person actually have the information you are looking for*? If, for example, the person has been recommended to you as someone who has a lot of old songs, is that information correct? I once went to see a woman on such a lead, only to have her show me a pile of old sheet music on top of the piano while admitting that she herself did not sing. On another occasion I went to see a man who told me he had known Lawrence Doyle, only to discover that he had been born the year Doyle died. I should add that in this case the man turned out to know a lot of Doyle's songs and had heard a lot about him from his parents and older neighbors, which made him a very valuable informant anyhow. It simply meant that his eyewitness accounts were something less than that. (By the way, I never "confronted" this informant with what I knew, which would have been to call him a liar. I simply kept what I knew in mind.)

Assuming that the prospect has the information you seek, your second question can follow: *Is this person willing and able to share that information with you*? You may find people who, for any one of a number of reasons or for no apparent reason at all, are simply not interested in talking with you. You may also find people who, no matter how hard you try to persuade them or what assurances you offer them, clearly want to avoid talking with you. It may be that the person is too busy, although I have usually found that "too busy" means "not interested." But under any circumstances, if the person does not want to talk with you, that is that. Several times, by the way, I have found that a reluctant informant will be less reluctant after a while, especially if he knows I have talked to other people in the area. Try checking back with such sources from time to time in order to give them "progress reports," as it were. Sometimes that is all that's needed. Finally, there may be no question about the person having the information, and he may be willing enough to talk with you, but he may not be physically or mentally able to help you. If the person is very deaf, and you have a tendency to mumble, perhaps someone else should interview this informant. I remember a man who knew Larry Gorman quite well, and he was perfectly willing to talk with me, but he was too senile to be able to tell me much; no matter what questions I asked, he would talk about whatever came into his head, which was never anything about Larry Gorman.

It is a good thing to remember—and all too easy to forget—that this decision-making is a two way street, that the informant is also deciding whether he or she wants to talk with you. After all, the whole business is an investment of time and energy on the informant's part just as it is on yours, and once there is an agreement to go ahead you can be sure that it is based on a mutual feeling that there is something in it for each of you. You need not worry about this matter too much, but do spend a few moments looking at the situation from the informant's point of view. It may be that he feels he has something of value to tell both you and the world, in which case it would not be surprising if the informant sought you out rather than the other way around. Several men have sent me lists of songs they knew, and one woman had her granddaughter come tell me that she was worried she was going to die and her songs would die with her. On the other hand, it may be that the informant, pleased with the prospect of being able to talk of the old days, has decided that you will be a good listener. It is difficult, sometimes, for a younger person to imagine the loneliness of old age and the release from it a series of interviews—meaning a series of visits—may represent. For some informants, the most important aspect of the interview is companionship, the simple joy of sharing a common space with another human being for even a little while. I am not, of course, suggesting that you interview a poor informant because it will be good therapy, only that you take a moment to understand what an informant's motivations may be, and do your best to accommodate them.

Such understanding may also help you deal with the prospective informant who is reluctant to be interviewed. The informant may feel that you will be using him, that you will make a lot of money out of this and where does he come in? If you are a student, you can answer such reluctance by explaining that you are working on an assignment or a paper. If you are not, you will simply have to offer the best explanation possible. I can say, however, that while I have found informants who were quite incredulous about my taking all this trouble if I *wasn't* going to make something out of it, they simply accepted my story and that was that. But if payment has not proved to be a problem, modesty has, and that brings us to consider a pretty basic matter.

The layman's conception of history (and, sadly, that of too many historians) has been so conditioned by the "great man/significant event" approach that it is frequently difficult for an ordinary mortal to believe that anyone is really interested in unremarkable him. "Nothing important ever happened to me," says a man who worked in the lumberwoods all his long life. "I never did anything," says a woman who brought up a family of seven in a mill town on a millhand's salary. Frequently this demurral is rather *pro forma,* the prospect needing only to be coaxed a little—and expecting to be. But occasionally it represents a sense of privacy or a conviction that life is something one lives, not talks about, so strong that you will not be able to overcome it. Naturally, if you encounter such convictions (and I have) you will have to accept them gracefully, no matter how senseless they seem. But this necessity does not arise very often.

Usually, once the prospective informant understands that you really have not made a mistake, that you *are* interested in what he or she can tell you, you are set.

There is a corollary to the modesty problem: words come easily to some people, not so easily to others. Probably the first people you will be referred to will be the good talkers, the "character," who "knows a million of 'em," the man who "will talk your leg off." They may be fine informants, but if we believe in the non-elitist approach to art and history—and that is one of the things this manual is all about—should we depend on the loquacious only? The tape-recorded interview is the best technique we have ever had for reaching out into the great silences and making them articulate, but God forbid that we let the glib do all the talking! I am not recommending that we should seek out the dull or the half-witted; they are even more exceptional than the glib. Nor am I recommending that we should avoid the good talker. All I am saying is that if we are out to record some aspect of the lives of common men and women, we should be less concerned with whether a prospective informant is articulate than with whether he has the experience we are interested in. If he has that experience, there is a lot we can do to help him tell about it. But that is a subject for a later section.

When should you bring up the business of the tape recorder? If you are reasonably certain that the prospect will respond positively to the idea, you can bring it up in your initial letter when you explain all about what you are doing. The great advantage of this method is getting everything out in the open to begin with, and I am coming more and more to believe that it is a good plan. But since neither I nor my students have done this as a rule, I still offer my standard advice: wait until the end of the preliminary interview, especially if you feel that the prospect may be at all shy about it. Assure yourself that the prospect will be a good informant; make arrangements for your first interview; then bring up the tape recorder ("By the way, I'll be bringing a tape recorder. That way I won't have to bother you by taking notes all the time, and we'll be sure we get it right when I write it all down later on. O.K.?"). Very seldom will there be any serious objection that you cannot overcome with a little reassurance and gentle persuasion.

If, however, your informant refuses to let you use the tape recorder, there is an alternative to calling the whole thing off. Make your appointment anyhow, and when you come to do the interview just start taking notes (bring the tape recorder with you but leave it out in the car). At some point, after some desperate note-taking and a few yelps like "Hold it" or "Would you repeat that again," request permission once more to use the tape recorder ("It'll be more accurate than my notes and a whole lot less bother for you", etc.). Sometimes this tactic works, and sometimes an informant may agree to let you use the tape recorder "next time." If the informant still refuses, though, and the refusal sounds final, you will have to decide whether it is worth continuing the series by taking notes and writing them up afterwards or whether it would be better to move on to work with someone else.

There will come a time when you will be tempted to record secretly, without the informant's knowledge or permission. It will be surprisingly easy to justify this action to yourself: the informant doesn't really "understand" how "important" this all is, you want to get the material "in its natural context," you don't want the tape recorder to "intrude" and spoil the "intimacy" of your conversation, etc.—all in the name of some high-sounding cause or entity like "scholarship." Learn early on to recognize the symptoms of this end-justifying-means distemper, and let your response be simple: *Don't do it.* It is an invasion of privacy, a betrayal of confidence, and a very shabby way for one human being to treat another. Again, *don't do it.*

As a corollary to the foregoing, always be sure the prospective informant is aware of what is going to happen to the material you are gathering. Don't claim that the tape is simply something between the two of you and that it will be destroyed later on (unless, of course, that is literally true). Make it clear that the tapes will be preserved in an archives. If you find that this puts the prospect off, try to determine what the problem is and offer reasonable assurances. We will have more to say about these assurances later, but for the moment don't make any promises neither you nor your archives can keep.

It is very helpful, both in your initial contact and in your preliminary interview, to mention how you came by the informant's name ("I'm interested in lumbercamp cooking, and Charlie Dinsmore said you'd be a good person to talk to, because you'd cooked in the woods as far back as he could remember . . . "). The combination of credential and testimonial is a wonderful ice-breaker. Take advantage of it whenever you can.

There comes, finally, the question of whether a completely separate preliminary interview is always and absolutely necessary. Can't you achieve the same results more efficiently over the phone? Yes, of course you can, especially if you already know the prospective informant or if you are working on familiar ground. And it is possible to combine the preliminary interview and the first interview ("Well, I've got the tape recorder right out in the car. What do you say we get started right now?"). I have done so frequently, especially when time is limited and I am working away from home. The sequence I have suggested—initial contact, preliminary interview, first interview —is simply a model I have found extremely workable, not only for myself but for my students as well, and as a model it can be adjusted to suit local circumstances, so long as the ground is covered and the spirit is fulfilled.

In sum, then, once you have determined that the prospective informant has the information you are looking for and that he or she is both willing and able to share it with you, you are ready to move ahead.

Advance Preparations

Before you go for your first interview, you should try to find out as much about your informant as you can. This does not mean that you should snoop or ask a lot of questions at the local store. I can think of no quicker way of getting off on the wrong foot. It simply means that you should check out obvious things like the feature article he mentioned that was written on his life in the local newspaper last year. If the informant has written a book, you should at least be acquainted with it, and ideally you should read it, especially if you are going to do more than just one or two interviews. If someone else has interviewed this informant, check those interviews. All these things will keep you from asking questions that have already been thoroughly answered, save you time and money, and show the informant you are serious about what you are doing.

Do a little map work too, especially if you are unfamiliar with the areas you and your informant will be talking about. What rivers are nearby? What lakes? What are the neighboring towns? A gas station road map is a big help, but if you want more detail, the U.S. Geological Survey ("Topographic") maps are excellent, giving the names of hills, coves, creeks, etc. (You can purchase them at almost any good university bookstore and at many sporting goods stores too.) You need not commit *all* this detail to memory, but you will be surprised how much even a cursory knowledge of the lay of the land will help you.

If one of the things you will be talking about is some local event of more or less note, find out what you can about it ahead of time. A local history may give you a good summary of it; there may even be an easily available newspaper account. In addition, if you are going to be interviewing someone whose main experience was in some particular occupation, you should familiarize yourself as well as you can with the outlines and terminology of that occupation, not so that you can impress the informant with your wisdom but so that you will have at least some idea what he is talking about and some conception of what might be worth asking questions about. I remember one young girl, interviewing an old woodsman, who asked what they cut down the trees with. "Well, girlie," he said with a kind of amused contempt, "we used an ax, that's what we used!" Girlie looked him right in the eye: "Poll or double-bit?" she said. You could feel his attitude change. "Well, mostly poll axes, but later on . . . ." It comes down to this: The more you know about your informant's life, work, and times, the better equipped you will be to carry on the interviews—and the more you will enjoy your work!

Should you prepare a list of questions you want to ask? Unequivocally I say yes, but never let them get in your way in the interview itself. A list of questions, even a general list of subjects you intend to cover, will help immensely, especially if you are not an old hand at interviewing, just so long as you don't get locked into it by checking things off or reading directly from it. Part of your advance preparation should certainly be to plan what it is you hope to talk about, and even to note down some specific questions. More about this later on.

Take plenty of tape along with you, ideally brand-new tape. Few interviews go beyond a couple of hours, which is no more than you could get on one tape, but always take at least twice as much tape as you think you will need. And before you set out, take a moment to number a couple of tapes ahead of time. Write this number right on the reel on the side that is up when you put the tape on the supply spindle. You can do this by pasting on a label, scratching it into the reel with a knife point or a nail, or writing it on with a felt tip pen (one that will write on smooth plastic!). Write the number on the box too, and include this number in all opening and closing announcements on the tape. Don't wait until later to put these numbers on; at the very latest, number the reels as you put them on the machine.

Use any numbering system that makes sense to you. You can simply number the tapes 1, 2, 3, . . ., or you can include the year (which is what I have always done: 80.1, 80.2, etc.). You can include the specific date (11/17/80 #1) or some combination of the informant's name, the date, and the number (Charlie 11/17/ #2). It doesn't matter how you do it, so long as you are consistent and the system makes sense to you (which assumes it will make sense to others). Of course, this number will go on your catalog too—one more simple way of keeping things straight. It will also help the archives staff later on, even though the archives will assign its own numbers to your tapes later. But don't try and use their system; in fact, it will help if your system is clearly different.

Since you have now done your homework and know your equipment, you are all set to go, right? Wrong. Make a last minute check. Have you enough tape? Have you got the mike (did you leave it on your desk when you were "playing the game" last night? Well, did you?)? Batteries? How about the plug-in cord (and, ideally, an extension cord)? Have you a pad and a pencil with an eraser (almost certainly you will need them)? Test your equipment just before you leave, because you may find that overnight, as W.C. Fields said, "Things happened!" I would suggest you test it by recording an advance announcement just before you set out. Let a good minute of tape go by blank (say 20-30 digits on the little counter), then make an announcement modeled on the following: "This is Friday, September 29, 1980, and I am on my way to interview Mr. John O'Connor of Edinburg, Maine, about the days when he used to work on the Argyle Boom. My name is Thurlow Blankenship and this is my tape number 80.3." That is, give the date (and the *year*), the name and address of the informant, what (in a very general way) you plan to talk about, who you are, and the number of the tape. Now play it back. This will allow you to get some necessary information on the tape and check your equipment at the same time.

And so, as Dr. Williams said to his townspeople, "Go now / I think you are ready." Or as ready as you will ever be. Go on. It's going to be great.

The Diary or Journal

Of all the tasks required of a good field worker, I find that keeping a journal is the toughest. I come home from an interview, and either I am tired or I must get immediately to other things or—most likely—both; consequently, the journal doesn't get written. I have good journals for less than half of my field work over the past twenty years, and I have had frequent occasion to regret that, because all too often the data I need when writing is just the sort of thing I would have put in my journal! But the fact that I have sinned and suffered the consequences makes me the ideal advocate for virtue: keep a journal, and keep it up to date.

It makes little difference what form you keep it in. I have found stiff-cover spiral notebooks workable, while I know one field worker who prefers to type his notes out and keep them in three-ring loose-leaf binders (his notes are absolutely a model of completeness too). It may be that the archives where you will be depositing your tapes has specific requirements of its own, and you can save yourself some trouble by inquiring ahead of time about this matter. Most likely, though, anything you turn in will be accepted. The two important things are to maintain the journal in a form that will make it easy for you to keep current, and to have some consideration for whoever in years to come may wish to refer to it, which is to say keep it dated, clear as to persons and places, and legible.

What should go into the journal? In addition to the sort of information I have suggested in the preceding paragraph, you should enter almost any information that will help us appreciate what went on. Where does the informant live? Describe the neighborhood. Describe his home or the place where you conducted the interview. Were there many books around? Was there a rug on the floor? Pictures on the wall (and what kind of pictures)? How was he dressed? Do you think he "got dressed up" for the occasion of the interview? Was his wife around? What effect did her presence have on the interview? Did the informant seem to accept the tape recorder, or did it seem to make him a little nervous? Did he keep glancing over at it, for example? How were you feeling about the whole situation? Were you nervous, and if you were do you think that bothered him? If you were ill or excessively tired, say so. It might help a lot to know that there was a picture on the wall that you found both fascinating and disturbing, and it would certainly help to know that you had the distinct feeling that at several points in the interview the informant was trying to get your goat. It is all but impossible to include too much, but as a guide for what to include or not include, simply ask yourself if this or that bit of information would help anyone listening to the tape or reading the transcript to make better use of it.

I have said that I am apt to get behind in this matter of keeping a journal. Lately, I have been trying a new technique: I keep a small cassette recorder with me. Then, while driving home from an interview, or immediately after I get home, I simply talk out my journal. Later, as soon as I have time, I transcribe my comments. In this way, since I am dictating while the experience is very fresh in my mind, my journals are more accurate and detailed. The only problem I foresaw was that I might never get around to transcribing my entries, but so far I have avoided that trap. And—most important— I am keeping up to date.

The Interview

Not only would it be pretentious for me to try and give a full treatise on interviewing here, it would be impossible. All I will do is give some technical advice that will help to make the recorded interview a more functional part of the whole process, and offer some suggestions on techniques I have used.

In order for the sort of interviewing we are concerned with to be as successful and useful as possible, there is a basic concept you should keep in mind: You are not holding a *dia*logue but always a *tri*alogue, with the tape recorder itself as the third party. Too much interviewing is done with the dialogue structure in mind, the tape recorder being relegated to a kind of catch-as-catch-can eavesdropper role. The interview, for example, is held in a noisy restaurant, and the mike is simply placed on the table next to the sugar bowl. The resultant tape will be of some use to the interviewer as a kind of stenographic record of what went on, but it will not offer much to the rest of us. To be sure, there will be times when valuable information can be recorded only under extremely bad conditions, but nine times out of ten such conditions are avoidable. Think of the microphone as the representative of a number of people (transcribers, listeners, future scholars) who for one reason or another are extremely interested in what is being talked about, then treat it with the consideration its constituency deserves. Everything I have to say about such things as mike placement, announcements, testing, using photographs, and cataloging is based on this trialogue concept.

While no one should become overly concerned about it, your interviews will be much easier to listen to and transcribe if you can learn to reassure the informant that you are listening without continually saying "uh-huh" or its equivalent. Try simply nodding or smiling. The desirability of this silence on your part will be obvious when you come to transcribe your first interview, but while some will find it easy to keep quiet, others will find it almost impossible. It is not an important enough matter to insist on. It is merely one of those trialogue considerations, and it does help to be mindful of your own verbal tics.

In no sense should anything I have said be construed to mean that I consider the chief end of interviewing to be the making of beautiful tapes. That would require treating the tape recorder as the most important of the three participants in the discussion (more ridiculous than ignoring it completely, leading to such monstrosities as "Into the mike, please," or "Can't you speak more clearly, Mr. Jones?"). I do, however, believe that the tape should be as good as it can be under the circumstances, and the trialogue rather than the dialogue-cum-eavesdropper concept will work to that end.

That leads us to the formality/informality problem. Some people feel that the little formalities I have been and will be suggesting spoil the "intimacy" of the interview, working against the easy give-and-take of conversation and putting the informant on guard. There is something to that impression, but it is usually exaggerated, just as the idea that the introduction of a tape recorder into an interview will cause the informant to "freeze-up" is exaggerated (and such objections are usually raised by people with little or no experience in the actual situation). Informality is desirable, but the fact is that we are talking about an *interview,* not a conversation. You are gathering, and the informant providing, information to be processed and stored, and while you should certainly work to keep things relaxed and friendly, you are *not* simply "having a nice chat." You are doing a job of work, and the informant knows that just as well as you do. *You* won't forget that the tape recorder is there; don't expect *him* to (even if he is a good enough actor to evince surprise that "that thing's been going" all the time). And if your telling him what will happen to the tapes puts him on guard, maybe he *should* be a little on guard. However, ninety-four per cent of the time this "stiffening" will not become a problem. All will go easily, and you will wonder what the fuss was about.

I have already suggested that you test your equipment just before you leave home by putting an opening announcement on tape. I always do, but even so, I always repeat the announcement in the informant's presence, largely because it is a good ice-breaker. The informant and I will usually be chatting about something while I set up the machine, place the mike, and so on. Then, when I am ready to begin the interview, I pick the mike up and say something like, "Well, let's get started." Then I speak directly into the mike, not looking at the informant at all, while I say, "This is Friday, September 29, 1980, and I am up in Argyle, Maine, in the home of [*now I look up at the informant*] Ernest Kennedy, and we're going to be talking about the days when he was a river-driver. My name is Sandy Ives and this is my tape 80.3." Then I put the mike back in its place, sit back and relax, and continue: "O.K., now that's taken care of. Now . . . " That is to say, I involve myself with the machine to begin with, then I involve the informant, and the interview is suddenly under way. I try to do it all in an offhand, diffident way. At the same time, I have made it unmistakably clear that the interview has begun.

From the outset, you should make certain that the informant understands what is going to happen to the tapes of the interview and that you get at least some acknowledgment of that understanding on the tape. From a strictly legal point of view, this acknowledgment has no value (that is, it does not constitute a "release"), but we at the Northeast Archives feel it shows our good intentions. You must tell the informant three basic things: that the tapes will be preserved, that people will be able to listen to them, and that he will be asked to sign a release at the end of the interview. I suggest some variation of the following, but try not to memorize it. Put it in your own words:

> I just want to tell you what's going to happen to these tapes we'll be making. They will be kept permanently in the Northeast Archives at the University of Maine. Then anyone who wants to find out how river-driving was done here on the Penobscot can learn by hearing about it from someone who actually did it himself. After the interview, I'll be asking you to sign a release, which will simply say that you're willing to have us use the material in this way. Is that O.K.?

If the informant has any questions or hesitations, now is the time to get them settled. If he wants to restrict the material somehow, you can explain whatever your archives' policy is in this regard and try to work out something satisfactory. But do not suggest the possibility of restrictions; let it come from the informant, if it comes at all.

There are two ways of getting the informant's acknowledgement on tape. First of all, you could simply explain the policy to him while the tape is running, just after you make your opening announcement. Or you could explain it all during your preliminary interview, or while you are setting up the tape recorder. If you do it this latter way, then all you need on the tape is something like, "O.K., now I explained about how we'll be keeping the tapes and about the release, didn't I?" and the informant's affirmative answer.

You may want to check your equipment a few minutes into the interview. To that end, start off with something inconsequential and eminently interruptible, just to get the informant talking for a few sentences. This will give you a chance to check your VU meter for level. Once you think the settings are about right, you can just go ahead. But if you have any doubts about how your equipment is performing, you can simply say, "Excuse me, I just want to make sure this machine is working properly." Then rewind a little—just enough to tell you what you want to know—and play it back. Once you are satisfied, put the machine back in *record* mode and go ahead with the interview. (I italicize *record,* because I know of a case where the interviewer just said "O.K." and blithely completed the interview with the recorder in *play* mode. Believe me, that was one angry interviewer when he got home!).

Since tape has a way of running out just when you need it most, you should know how long each side of a tape or cassette will run at the speed you are employing. An occasional glance at the supply reel will be enough to tell you when you need to turn the tape over. But look at the machine, not your watch. Any time you check your watch, your informant will notice (as you would notice if he checked his) and be likely to conclude that you are either bored or in a hurry. When you see only a little tape left, simply explain that fact to the informant, and make the change. When you start up again, leave about a minute (say 20 to 30 digits) of blank tape on the new side, and make an announcement like the one with which you began the interview, only saying that this is the *continuation* of an interview, not the beginning of a new one. Since it sometimes happens in an archives that a tape will by mistake wind up wrong-end out on a reel, this little announcement could save the archives staff a lot of time and trouble later on.

Remember, a tape or cassette only has two sides. When you flip it over, keep in mind that you have done so, and when you come to the end of the second side, *change tapes.* It is very easy to flip the tape again and accidentally start recording over on the first side, erasing the beginning of your interview or whatever you had recorded on side one. And when you get home and see what you've done, the self-anger and sense of stupid frustration you will feel will surpass even the time you locked the keys in the car! To guard against such a blunder, mark your take-up reel distinctively on both sides, or, if you have a cassette machine, make sure the cassette sides are marked A and B, and always start with the A side.

How you conduct the interview will be largely a function of what it is you are looking for, and here I find it useful to distinguish between performance and discourse interviews. An example should make the point. Say your informant is a woman who has been recommended to you as knowing a lot of songs. Now a song is a discrete entity, having a very clear beginning, middle, and end. Frequently, you can even ask for one by name ("Can you sing 'Barbara Allan'?") or by type ("Do you know any other pirate songs?"), and the response will be the *performance* of a specific song. She will *sing* and you will listen, and—making allowance for the change of context —that is almost certainly the way the song would have been presented in its natural context (i.e. outside the interview context): a singer, a performer, presenting the item to an audience of sorts. By the time the interview is over, you will be able to say something like, "I collected twelve songs from Mrs. Callahan this afternoon."

Collecting "items" like songs or stories from people who are considered singers or storytellers (either by others or by themselves or both) is oftentimes a pretty easy business, once you have gotten them to agree to the idea in the first place—and frequently enough that is far from a hard thing to do. The informant knows very clearly what is expected—a series of performances—and all you have to do is sit quietly and listen like a good audience. Even if the informant is not an acknowledged performer, the situation will still be much the same. It may be a little more difficult to get such a person to perform ("I never was much of a singer"), but once it is clear you are looking for specific *items* he or she knows ("—but my father was a real singer, and I guess I heard most of them often enough so I know them—"), you are well on your way ("—and I guess I could sing 'em for you somehow."). The interview will still be a series of performances.

You will recall that I described the interview situation as a trialogue. In the performance-oriented interview, the informant will be performing for both you and the tape recorder. You as interviewer will have a triple role. During the performances you will be the attentive, extremely attentive, audience; between performances you will be a kind of low-key master of ceremonies; and all the time you will be a sound engineer, paying considerable attention to both the equipment and the ambience, which is to say that the tape recorder itself will assume considerable importance. You may do "test takes" and spend time monitoring the performance through earphones or fussing with exact mike placements (you may even bring in exotic equipment like mike booms). If there are other people in the room, you may even find yourself "hushing" them. In brief, roles will be very clear. The recording of performances makes perfect sense all around. In fact, it seems as though that is what one *ought* to be recording.

On the other hand, rather than looking for specific items, you may be more interested in a way of life, a process, an occupation, or some historical or legendary event or person. You may simply want to interview someone with nothing more specific in mind than getting a life history of the most rambling sort, either for its own sake or with an eye to editing it all into an autobiography some day. What is important is not performance but *discourse* and the information carried by that discourse, and the roles of the three trialogue participants will be quite different from what they would be for a performance-oriented interview. As the interviewer, you will be asking questions and actively eliciting information from the informant, who will be responding to your leads (at least in part). You will want to encourage the easy flow of information, and while some formality is inevitable and even desirable (as I said earlier, you are *not* just having a nice chat), you should do everything you can to keep the informant from feeling he is "on stage." To this end, you should pay as little attention as possible to the tape recorder and the mike, after seeing that both are well and unobtrusively placed, and you will be less concerned with maintaining an acoustically perfect ambience (hushing people, fretting when the telephone rings, etc.). In fact, if newcomers do interrupt the interview, you can take it as some indication that you have been successful in keeping it low-key and easy. They will not be embarrassed until they see the recorder. After all, a simple conversation seems like the sort of thing one ought *not* to be recording.

This is not to say that specific items of folklore will not surface in such interviews. They will crop up frequently, but still in the context of the general discussion. The informant may use proverbial comparisons ("That man was tougher'n a bag of hammers") or he may tell a joke (" 'Course that's like the two Irishmen was walking down the street and . . . ") to illustrate a point. (By the way, some of the best examples of traditional remedies I have ever collected have come to me in this way: "That ax jumped off that knot and cut my shin clean to the bone, but I just put some tobacco on it, and it healed all right.") He may also respond to your requests for specific items ("Well that was old Archie Stackhouse, and the way I heard it was he . . . "). The point is, though, that the material does not come to you as performance but as information. The informant may, in your opinion or in the opinion of others, be a good talker or even a "good storyteller," but the stories do not come for their own sake but rather as illustrations of a point or in response to a question. The specific items are not the important matter; the information they carry is.

Having made this distinction between performance and discourse, let me hasten to say that practically never will an interview be made up of one or the other exclusively. They are not polarities but rather the limits of a continuum, and any interview will contain elements of both. Ballad-singing is about as pure performance as you are apt to come across, yet in a song-collecting interview there probably (and hopefully) will be some discussion between the songs. On the other hand, the proverb is a very discursive or conversational genre, yet by the very fact that it calls attention to itself and the speaker it is to some extent performed. While most of the users of this manual will be conducting discursive interviews, there are very few folklorists who have not put in some time recording straight performances. Keeping the performance/discourse distinction in mind should help you understand what is going on in a particular interview and how you should behave in order to keep it going.[4]

One final word on performance interviews is in order, here. Since you will playing the audience role, try to determine what the performer expects of an audience. For example, I have found that in Maine and the Maritimes, singers are sometimes put off by people who appear to be listening too intently ("She just kept staring at me!"), who "relate" to the song too obviously (by swaying their bodies, smiling sincerely), or who join in on the refrains. Yet if a

4. For a good discussion of this performance/discourse continuum, see William Hugh Jansen, "Classifying Performance in the Study of Verbal Folklore," in *Studies in Folklore in Honor of Stith Thompson,* ed. W.E. Richmond (Bloomington: Indiana University Press, 1957), pp. 110–118.

man falters, I have found it is all right (especially in Irish communities) to say something like "Good for you, John." Generally, though, one sits there, silent, reserved, maybe looking at the floor, maybe not. It took me some time to learn the role, but I am awfully glad I did.

It may be helpful to keep yet another distinction in mind. Kenneth Goldstein distinguishes between natural and artificial contexts in folklore.[5] Here, there are essentially three criteria involved. In a natural context, the song or tale is presented *by* someone who would normally perform it, *for* people who would be the usual audience, and *at* a time and place when such performance would be expected. Any other context is an artificial one. The ideal, of course, is to study folklore in its natural context. For example, if one is studying children's games, he can simply spend a lot of time watching children at play from some vantage point where his presence will not disturb them or affect their actions. In this way he would see the games in their completely natural context. Should he make himself obvious (for instance, by standing nearby and taking notes or using a tape recorder or camera), he could be almost certain that his presence would affect what is going on, and the context would therefore be to some extent artificial. If he moved off the playground completely and spent his time interviewing children about what games they play, he would be operating in a still more artificial context, and if he interviewed adults about games they used to play when they were children, he would have gone one step further.

Obviously, the techniques discussed in this manual are entirely aimed at collecting in an artificial context. My own work is a perfect case-in-point. I have written extensively on lumbercamp songs, yet I have never lived in a lumbercamp nor heard an old come-all-ye sung along the deacon seat. All my collecting has been done from men who *had* been woodsmen themselves and used to sing these songs in camp or remembered hearing them sung there. And the interviews were conducted years after the fact, in kitchens and parlors all over the Northeast. Clearly, then, I have had to rely on material gathered outside its natural context.

Yet the artificial context may be the only one in which you *can*

5. Kenneth S. Goldstein, *A Guide for Field Workers in Folklore* (Hatboro, Pa.: Folklore Associates, 1964), pp. 80–87.

gather your data, because the natural context no longer exists (there are, for instance, no more all-winter lumbercamps). In such a situation, you can reconstruct the natural context by asking all sorts of questions about, say, what life was like in an all-winter lumbercamp, when singing took place, who sang, who listened, and so forth. Even if you can still gather data in its natural context, there will always be supplementary material that can be best covered in a follow-up interview. Say, for instance, you have recorded a country/ western singer's performance at a local bar—certainly a natural context.[6] The next day you go to his home, interview him in his living room, and, in the process, get him to sing over several of the songs he sang the night before. Obviously, then, the interview context is by its very nature an artificial one, yet there is nothing wrong with that, so long as you don't fool yourself or attempt to fool others about what it is you are doing or have done. Anyone who makes pronouncements about a form he has never observed in its natural context must understand the limitations of his pronouncements and make those limitations clear to his readers.

As the interview moves along, keep this rule in mind: *The tape should be as complete and accurate a record of the interview as you can possibly make it.* Remember that a tape recording has no visual aspect, and many things that will be clear to you, since you were there at the time, will not be clear to someone else who was not there. (Chances are they will not even be clear to *you* some years, months, or even days later.) Keep the trialogue concept in mind, thinking of the tape recorder as the *blind* third party, for whom all gestures, pointings, and the like must be interpreted. In this way, some of the visual material can be captured right on the tape. If a

6. Neil Rosenberg has suggested that in recording performances in their natural context, one should place the microphone where it can pick up the full ambience of sound—audience coming and going, people talking and ordering drinks, pinball and cigarette machines operating, etc. See his article, "Studying Country Music and Contemporary Folk Music Traditions in the Maritimes: Theory, Techniques, and the Archivist," *Phonographic Bulletin* 14 (May, 1976), 18–21. This has been reprinted in his booklet, "Country Music in the Maritimes: Two Studies," Memorial University of Newfoundland Department of Folklore, Reprint Series, No. 2 (1976). His comment is worth quoting in full: "Whenever possible," he said, "I recorded events: Dances, fiddle contests, jam sessions, house parties, radio sessions, and rehearsals. In most of these situations I used an omnidirectional microphone and set the recorder at slow speed, so as to record the total audio event." (reprint, p. 15).

man gestures that something was "about that long," you can say, "About three feet, eh?" Or if he says, "He was over there, and I was right here," drawing it out in the air for you, you can interject, somewhere, "That'd be about fifty yards away on your left, then?" Still, such gesturing frequently becomes a problem when someone is explaining how to do something like notching a log or building a cabin. Occasionally, you can get the informant to draw a picture for you (one reason why you should always have paper and pencil at hand), or you can draw it out for him and ask, "Is this the way you mean?" Then you can include these drawings as part of your catalog, indicating in the text just where the drawing comes into play (for example, [*See drawing no. 1.*]). You can sometimes explain extraneous noises right on the tape, too ("Wow, that jet sounded awful low" . . . "Is that a chain saw out there?"), but at the very least you should explain all such matters in your catalog.

If you feel that what is being conveyed by gesture is crucial, don't hesitate to slow the interview down to the point where you can interpret the gestures properly ("Now whoa, let's see now, there were three of those piers maybe fifty feet apart standing in a line out from shore and you say you were standing halfway between the second and third?"). It is very likely that at moments like this your informant will be looking for reassurances from you by saying "Y'see?" or "Know what I mean?" more often than usual, and you should steel yourself against giving such reassurances when you really do *not* "see" or when you know the explanation will not be clear to the tape recorder. But sometimes it is all but impossible to slow things down, in which case make a note to yourself to write out —using your own words and diagrams—a good description of the process in question and then ask about it in a subsequent interview. This technique will give your informant a chance either to approve or to correct your description, which will go a long way toward clarification.

It may be that a tape recording can in no way convey the process in question, or can only do so at the price of fantastic verbal contortions on your part, while a movie, a videotape, or even a series of still photographs could do the job very simply. It might be barely possible, for instance, to describe a series of dance steps in words, but it would be much more worthwhile to get a good videotape of the same steps. Showing such a videotape to an informant and then taping his comments on what he sees might be extremely valuable, just as a description of a whittled object would be made more valuable by some accompanying photographs. But the incorporation of visual aids into an interview raises its own problems, which we will take up at a later time.

As a rule, you should keep the tape running throughout the entire interview. Don't turn it on and off to "save tape" or to avoid recording material that seems "irrelevant." For one thing, you may not be a very good judge of what is irrelevant or unimportant. Besides, such on-the-spot editorializing can be insulting. The person you are talking to may feel that what he is telling you is very relevant and important, and no matter how bright and politely interested you manage to look, he will realize that you have turned the recorder off. Then, when he starts talking about something you think is important again, you will have to stop him or miss recording the beginning of the story—and that may be very important. It is simplest, politest, and generally best just to leave the tape running and not get involved in this kind of judgment.

On the other hand, there will certainly be times when you should turn the machine off temporarily. If your informant is called out of the room for a minute to answer the phone, or some such matter, or if company arrives and all attention is turned that way for a while, it makes sense to stop recording. Sometimes you can get an explanation of the interruption right on the tape ("Mr. O'Connor has to go outside and talk to a delivery man, so I'm shutting down for a minute"), or you can enter it in your catalog later on, along with a statement of about how long the tape was off. Then when you begin again, you can simply mention the subject of the informant's last remarks and continue.

What do you do when your informant tells you to "shut the damn thing off for a minute"? The answer is simple: *shut it off.* Don't spend time trying to get permission to leave it running, and certainly, never play tricks like leaving it on when you say you have turned it off. Confidence and trust are too important to be trifled with, and you should do nothing that might make the informant unsure either of you or of his own judgment. This is especially true if the idea of being interviewed is something new to him, in any way, or if you are a stranger. Turn the machine off—quickly, calmly, and cheerfully. It may be that what you are told off the record is material you would just as soon leave off the record. That is the way it will work out most of the time, which means there is no real problem and you are both glad the tape was stopped. But if the material is something you *are* interested in, you *do* have a problem, and it will require tact to solve it.

The chances are that it will become perfectly obvious why you were asked to turn the machine off. The informant may even volunteer the reason, or, if he does not, and if you are puzzled, you can ask. In any event, there are two classic explanations for reluctance of the "turn-that-thing-off" variety: the material in question is felt to be either inappropriate or threatening.

The informant may be concerned that a story is "too foolish" to go on the tape, or that it has "nothing to do with what we're talking about," or (and this is a very common concern) that it is "off-color." In a sense, then, he is trying to be considerate and not waste your tape, which leaves it up to you to convince him that the material is anything *but* foolish or irrelevant. I have sometimes found that this reluctance is not only very superficial, it is a feint on the informant's part to determine whether I really want "that sort of thing" (it frequently works this way in connection with off-color material). Sometimes you can spot this tactic ahead of time. I remember one man who, having just sung me seven or eight wonderful old ballads, suddenly chuckled and said that "maybe we better not put this one on." I sensed the feint and encouraged him to go ahead, which he did. The song was riotously funny, but, since he had been singing serious ballads all afternoon, he wanted assurance that I would not object to "such a foolish thing." He got it, and I got the song.

It may be, however, that the informant's reluctance has deeper roots, such as his not wishing to speak ill of the dead or fearing that whatever is said will "get back" to the person under discussion or his family. The informant may fear (rightly or wrongly) getting involved in libel or slander, or he may simply not be sure enough of his information to want to go on record about it. In these situations, the informant is trying to protect himself, which means you must find a way to allay his concern (assuming, of course, that you do not share it). Don't hurry the situation. Make a mental note of the material (nothing more, at least not in front of the informant), and come back to it later. I would even recommend waiting until a subsequent interview; it is surprising how reluctance fades as the informant comes to know and trust you. Even so, you may still have to offer some encouragement by explaining why this is just the sort of material you need, that it will not get back to or harm anyone, and so forth. You may even offer (if it seems necessary, and if your archives is willing) to restrict the material in some suitable way. Here, you will have to use your judgment, but remember two things. First, never offer well-meaning assurances you cannot make good. Second, do not commit either yourself or your archives to imposing restrictions on an interview that are patently in excess of what is needed simply to allay someone's concern over possible repercussions. The offer of restrictions should come as a last resort.

Who is "in charge" of the interview? Who controls the direction it takes? Since you know what it is you want to find out, the simplest answer is that you are the one who will guide it, but it doesn't always work that way, nor should it. At the beginning, assume that you are going to direct the interview, but your informant may have ideas of his own and will turn to things he wants to talk about. Be conscious of what is happening, and listen carefully. He may seem to get off on terrible tangents, but he may also be telling you about what he knows best, and you should explore that first. For example, I remember one ex-woodsman who led the discussion into the business of being a teamster, which obviously interested and excited him. The interviewer listened politely, then said, "Uh, yes, now I was asking you what the different buildings were in a camp. Would you . . . " She put the interview back where she wanted it and got answers to her questions, but the fire was out. Even his discussion of teaming in a later interview was less spirited. She should have gone with him and explored the teamster business when he wanted to talk about it and then come back to other matters later. So when it comes to the question of directing the interview, the answer is that you should, but be ready to let go intelligently.

There is another good reason for not being too insistent about directing the interview: sometimes the sequence in which the informant brings subjects up may be particularly revealing. A shift in subject, a sudden (or not so sudden) tangent—what brought it about? What suggested it? You ask about one thing and you get another: why? If, for example, you try to hold to a neat chronological sequence and your informant keeps breaking out of it, rather than becoming exasperated at his disorderliness, try asking yourself what order *he* might be following. I warn you against cheap psychologizing, but associations, avoidances, and substitutions can give you valuable information. Once again, it is a matter of letting go intelligently and (without insisting on an insight in every tangent) listening carefully.

Earlier on, I recommended the use of lists of topics you want to cover and questions you want to ask. It may be that you can pick up ready-made interview guides or questionnaires from your archives or from the project you are working on. There are several state guides available, and while they are obviously designed for use in their respective states, they are by no means entirely useless elsewhere.[7] Then there are the vast compendia like the Irish *A Handbook of Irish Folklore* and the British *Notes and Queries on Anthropology* (see the Bibliography), but none of these works will be any substitute for your own knowledge of your field of inquiry, especially your knowledge of what areas are not well known and need documentation. Never ask a question you do not understand yourself. That sounds self-evident, but it is one of the traps someone else's list of questions can lead you into. For instance, you should never ask a question such as, "Did you ever use a—a parbuckle—to yard logs?" when you don't even know what a yard is. Your informant will not be fooled, and you will just be confused and bored by his answers. This is not to say that you have to be an expert or that you should only ask questions to which you already have the answers. There will be many things that will not be clear to you, and you should certainly ask questions about them, but that is a different matter from not even understanding what the question itself means. The best ad-

7. See, for example, Jan Harold Brunvand, *A Guide for Collectors of Folklore in Utah* (Salt Lake City: University of Utah Press, 1971); George G. Carey, *Maryland Folklore and Folklife* (Cambridge, Md.: Tidewater Publishers, 1970); MacEdward Leach and Henry Glassie, *A Guide for Collectors of Oral Traditions and Folk Cultural Material in Pennsylvania* (Harrisburg: Pennsylvania Historical and Museum Commission, 1968). All three contain hints on collecting and a small anthology of examples of various folklore genres already collected in that state.

vice I can give on interview guides and pre-prepared questionnaires is that you should use them ahead of time to help you prepare your own list of questions. The very act of compiling such a list will help to fix the questions in your mind, *and that is where they should be.*

The second best bit of advice I can offer about using an interview guide is that you should be extremely careful about getting tied to it or excessively dependent upon it. Again, don't read questions from it; pay no attention to it while the informant is talking (never leaf through it or check things off), and don't for Heaven's sake let it take over the interview by becoming in your mind something to be "gotten through." You should not even consider getting through it a virtue!

Once you have the formalities of the opening announcement and the explanation of what will happen to the tapes out of the way, how do you get the interview itself started? A great deal will depend on what it is you are looking for and what your informant's expectations may be (what you said in your letter, what was discussed in the preliminaries, etc.). You will always have a reason for setting up an interview; we can take that for granted, but it may be a pretty vague or general reason. You may have an interest in logging and lumbering, and an informant who spent many years of his life as a woodsman, or you may be interviewing a woman to find out what it was like to spend fifty years as a farm wife in northern Aroostook County. Frequently you will be interested not in someone's whole life but in some specific segment of it, such as the years a woman might have spent as district nurse before her marriage, or what it might have been like to work in a cotton mill during the years the union was trying to get established there. The last of these is by far the most specific topic, but even so we can still describe it as a general area for questioning rather than a specific question. And the same would hold true if you were interviewing someone recommended as a great storyteller or singer of old songs. In short, with an informant and an area of interest, you have staked a claim; now you are ready to explore it.

I can suggest a model to follow, so long as we understand it to be nothing more than a model: begin general, become specific. Start by getting the basic biographical information, if that comes easily—age, place of birth, family, schooling, length of residence here and elsewhere, etc.—but don't insist on anything. These are useful ice-breaking questions, but if you find your informant becoming restive, move on to something else. Move into the list of possible questions you have made up, but be very alert to what it is he may want to talk about, and try to follow his leads wherever possible. In the beginning, it is just as important (perhaps even crucial) to show the informant that you are interested in him and the things he is interested in as it is to gather data. Call it a combination of "establishing rapport" and exploring, because it certainly is both. Let your interviews move, then, from the general and non-directed, with special attention to establishing rapport, to the controlled and specific, with continued attention to maintaining that rapport.

There is an exception to this approach that, on the one hand, is a very large one and, on the other, is not really an exception at all. If you have come to interview someone in regard to something very specific, don't waste a lot of time on generalities. Get right to it, especially if the informant knows why you have come, largely because it is the most natural thing to do. As a matter of fact, some of the best interviews I have ever conducted, and certainly some of the best interviews my students have conducted, have come about when we stood the model on its head. In this connection, it is time to talk about the principle of serendipity.

I have always found that field workers (especially novice field workers) do their best work when looking for something very specific, and frequently the more specific it is the better. I would never turn a student loose to go look for "folklore" or even "information" on old times. I would insist on a sharper focus, say "the fire of 1910," or "Old Dalton and his stories," or "bears and bear hunting," or "the Collins murder," and I recommend the same approach to readers of this manual. Such focussing is especially useful if you are working with virtual strangers in a strange area, because it gets the interview off to a good solid start: the informant knows what you are looking for, and you know what you want to ask. But (and here is the serendipity) as the interview progresses, keep your mind open for material you could not have known enough to ask for and may not even have dreamed existed.

Serendipity is the story of my life. While I was trying to learn all I could about songs of the Maine lumberwoods, I first heard of Larry

Gorman. While I was interviewing a man about Gorman, he told me about Joe Scott. And while I was gathering material for my book on Scott, I had a man tell me about Lawrence Doyle.[8] Two years later, a man I was interviewing about Doyle turned out to be a creditable fiddler and also introduced me to a whole cycle of tall tales told by and about yet another local character. At another time I had gone to collect songs from a man who had been described to me as a fine singer (he was, too), when a chance visitor happened to mention the name of a local poacher, about whom the singer proceeded to tell several stories (that poacher is the subject of my next book!). In each case I was looking for one thing; in each case I found something of value I had not expected. I could offer further examples, and I am sure other folklorists could easily duplicate my experience, but the point is made: know what you are looking for and go for it, but never let yourself be blind to other possibilities. The most interesting material of all may turn out to be what you catch out of the corner of your eye. This is the principle of serendipity, and it will always work in your favor, if you let it.

It is obvious why this approach *is* an exception to the general-to-specific model. But at the same time it is *not* an exception because it uses the specific search largely as an opener, a way in. Once you get beyond it, you are back to the model again in a very easy and natural way. When my students and I were compiling material for our book on Argyle Boom, we had several interviews with Ernest Kennedy, who had sorted and rafted logs there for years.[9] Some time after the project was completed, I was going over the catalogs of our interviews with Ernest and saw all kinds of little suggestions of further riches ("That was the spring after I came back from the Allagash" . . . "I was cooking that winter for my father up on Hemlock Stream . . . " etc.). I went back to see him, and while I have had at least forty hours of interview with him, the end is not yet in sight.

So much depends on who you are, who your informant is, and

8. For the story of my discoveries of these three songmakers, see my *Larry Gorman: The Man Who Made the Songs* (Bloomington: Indiana University Press, 1964), especially pages 2–7; *Lawrence Doyle: The Farmer-Poet of Prince Edward Island* (Orono: University of Maine Press, 1971), especially pages xv–xviii; *Joe Scott: The Woodsman Songmaker* (Urbana: University of Illinois Press, 1978), especially pages xxi–xxvii.

9. Ives, *Argyle Boom*.

the particular chemistry of your interaction, that it is almost impossible to give specific advice on how to conduct an interview once you have made your beginning. Some people are self-starters, talk easily, give lots of detail, move from one subject to another effortlessly, and in general need very little help from you, although you may want to keep the tangents from becoming too tangential. Others will require more work on your part, because for one reason or another they will not volunteer much. Such a person may know a lot and have a great fund of experience but find the words hard to come by. What can you do to help?

First, you can help by creating as easy and relaxed an atmosphere for the interview as is possible under the circumstances. Second, you can help by showing the informant that you really are interested in what he has to say and that you recognize its importance. My third suggestion is that you help with the kinds of questions you ask. One of the classic bits of advice is never to ask a question that can be answered by yes or no. It is good advice, but I find it devilishly hard to follow (Q: "Did you ever drive team?" A: "Sure") and not always that much of a problem so long as I remember to follow up (Q: "Where was that?" A: "Well, . . . "). That leads me to my fourth and most important suggestion: *probe.*

A probe is simply a device for eliciting more and better information in an interview, or, to put it another way, of helping your informant tell his story more completely. For example, among the kinds of answers you will get to your opening questions, especially in interviews on occupations, is what I call the "they" answer. You ask, "How would you go about building a road in the woods?" and the answer comes, "Well, the first thing they'd do would be to . . . " or "Well, first you'd . . . " Now there is nothing really wrong with that sort of answer; in fact you will get some excellent descriptions of tasks and processes in this form, because it is a very natural way to describe things. (As a matter of fact, it is probably the way *you* would describe a process you were familiar with yourself.) But when you are interviewing, don't let description stop there. Get your informant to describe his own particular and unique experience with this task or process.

Raymond Gorden's good book deals with the matter of probes at great length, and what I have to say will be much simpler and less systematic.[10] But if your informant has given you a good "they" answer, you can often get him to particularize by asking such questions as the following:

> "Did that ever happen to you?"
> "Did you ever do that yourself?"
> "Can you give me an example of that?"
> "Where was this? When?"
> "Wait a minute. I don't quite see how that worked. Now you say that . . . "

Sometimes a simple evincing of surprise will serve as a probe ("That many?" "Were they as big as all that?"), or a quizzical look or raised eyebrow may be enough.

One of the most effective probes—and it is a good deal more than that—is simple *silence*. Don't be afraid of silence, first of all; never feel that you have to keep talking. Try shutting up and see what happens. Learn to interpret whether a pause means that the informant has really finished what he has to say and is waiting for guidance from you, or if it means only that he is considering what to say next. Take your time in either case. If he is still thinking, your jumping in may prevent him from giving you further details; if he really is through, it might be that in the pause he will think of something *he* wants to say. Remember that the informant will be just as conscious of the silence as you are, and just as anxious to fill it). This is not to say there cannot—and will not—be *awkward* silences; it is just to say that silence can be useful.

Another valuable kind of probe is the question based on something said in an earlier interview ("Last time I was here you mentioned that, during the winter you worked up around Kennebago, you were on a hot yard. Now I'm not clear just what a *hot* yard was. Could you go into that a little for me?"). There are any number of things you can do with this sort of retrospective probe, like finding out where or when something took place, getting more details, or checking previous ones. It is an excellent kind of question because, among other things, it shows your informant that you have been paying attention to what he said and are really serious about your work. Conversely, nothing can alienate your informant like making

10. Raymond Gorden, *Interviewing: Strategy, Techniques and Tactics,* rev. ed. (Homewood, Ill.: Dorsey Press, 1975), pp. 422–444.

him go over the same ground again out of mere forgetfulness.

There is a special kind of retrospective question that violates my principle of being absolutely honest with your informant, but I have found it very useful. Frequently people have stories they tell about themselves or ways of narrating some personal experiences that make these narrations "set pieces." That is, they are favorite stories and have been told often enough in the past that they have become pretty well fixed in their structure and details. Such stories are often among the first an informant tells, or perhaps you can spot them because a third party will say something like, "Charlie, tell him the one about old George and the skunks." At any rate, however you recognize such material, it is an excellent idea to get that story two, three, or even several times. To begin with, you might simply ask the informant to tell you the story again. If you bring a friend with you, you might ask your informant if he would do you a favor and tell it to him. Or (and here is the "deception"), you can claim that the recording was not clear on that story, or it somehow did not record at all or even got erased, and would he please go over it again because it is just too good to lose? You will probably have no trouble getting him to repeat a favorite story, but if you do, well, I am certainly not going to tell you to say that which is not strictly true. But it would be nice to get that story again, wouldn't it?

I cannot overemphasize the importance of recording the same item more than once. If, for example, a man sings a song only once for you, he may leave a stanza out—accidentally or on purpose—yet cover the omission so smoothly that you would never notice it. Repeated singings on different occasions could reveal such omissions. Conversely, something that sounds like a mistake the first time through may turn out to be quite purposeful. If someone is telling a story, it may be that he has several ways of telling it, depending on who he is telling it for, when, where, and so on. If it is a narrative of his own experiences, it will be interesting to try to find out just how much of a "set piece" it really is, how fixed in form and detail. Naturally, all of us like to gather "new" material, and it is understandable if you chafe a bit when you hear "the same old thing" again. But if you are interested in oral tradition—if you are a folklorist, of course you are; if you are an oral historian, you should be!

—you must learn not only to accept repetition gracefully but even to seek it out on occasion.

By the way, this re-eliciting is also valuable for checking facts. In two different descriptions of an experience, do the men's names stay the same? Are the same numbers involved? Where did it take place? When? This process is not so much to see whether a man is telling the truth (though it can help determine that, if you have some doubts) as it is to discover what is important and what is not. For example, I had a man tell me about someone coming back from the dead as a big white dog to drive off some land speculators who were annoying his wife. The next time the man told the story, it involved a black dog. That variation does not invalidate his story; it just means that the color was an inconsequential detail for him.

How about "leading questions"? Some people call them "loaded questions," but whatever you call them they are questions in which you put words into your informant's mouth by framing your question in such a way that the response you want is perfectly clear. A gentleman who will be happier nameless was interviewing an elderly Micmac Indian, and the Indian told him something that had happened years ago. "Don't you think," said the interviewer, "that is a good example of the way the white man has exploited the Indian all these years?" "Yes sir!" came the reply, "it sure is." Stay away from that sort of futile exercise. It is tempting, and it makes you feel as though you are getting somewhere, but the results are worse than useless because they are misleading.

On the other hand, there is one kind of leading question I have used with considerable success: the *negative* leading question. I have found it especially useful in gathering biographical information, not about the informant but about some third party. If you ask, "What kind of a guy was he?" (and by the way that is still a perfectly decent way to begin, but listen very carefully to what is said and not said), you will probably be told that he was a pretty nice fellow. If you ask, "Was he a good man?" you will probably be told that he was indeed a good man. But if you come at it negatively, you can get interesting results. For example, while I was gathering material for a biography of the songmaker Joe Scott, I wanted to see how one informant who knew him well would react to a negative assessment of

Joe's character. "Look," I said, "I was talking to someone the other day, and he told me that Joe was just a damn nuisance around the camps." No one, in fact, had told me any such thing, but if my informant agreed with that assessment, he could say so without feeling that he had been the one to bring it up. If he did not agree, he would find it very easy to say so, and that is just what he did, vehemently. "No sir!" he said, and went on from there. You need not always invent such opinions, either. I knew that one man I was writing about had the reputation of being a thief. One informant telling me a lot about him was carefully avoiding that side of the story, until I remarked, "Couple of people told me he would have been a real fine guy but he couldn't stop stealing stuff." The reply came slowly, but smilingly: "Well, I wasn't going to say anything about that, but if you already know about it, yes . . ." Be judicious with the negative leading question. Use it only after you have used more standard methods, but it will sometimes stir things up just the right way.

The length of the interview will vary with each informant. I have gone on for several hours, and I have quit after ten minutes, depending upon whom I was talking to and what I was looking for. Still, I would offer this as a pretty good rule of thumb: one hour, give or take a little. It is not only that your informant may become tired; you will too, and an hour is about all either of you will want. You can always go back again, of course. In fact, you probably will be going back several times, and it is always better to stop too soon than to risk wearing out your welcome. But say transportation is a problem. You have traveled a hundred miles to see this man, and at the end of an hour you have just begun. Use your own judgement, but you might consider taking a break ("Look, we've been going at this for about an hour now, and I should go downtown and do a few errands, so why don't I come back after supper?"). That will give you a chance at least to listen to the interview so far and formulate some questions based on it.

How many interviews should you hold with one informant? Frequently you will need only one, but I have held as many as twenty, and others have gone well beyond that. The more I work at this game, though, the more I see a sort of minimum unit: *one interview and a follow-up,* which is to say two interviews. As I review my work, I find occasions where in my haste I neglected to have a follow-up interview, and almost every time I have had leisure to regret it. I find something I should have asked, something that needed clarification or amplification, but by then it is too late. That is why I suggest you should consider the follow-up interview as routine, and you should also consider it routine to review the first interview with some care before the follow-up. It would be ideal if you could make a complete catalog (or even a complete transcript, if transcripts are part of your program), but that is not always possible. However you review your interview, take careful notes on questions you want to ask. Thus, the minimum requirement for good technique involves four steps: advance preparation, the interview itself, a review of that interview, and a follow-up. If that leads to more interviews, fine; if it does not, you have a good solid document nonetheless.

If you think it was tough getting started, wait until you try and conclude a series of interviews. You may find that you have come to know your informant rather well, and now you both face the prospect of not seeing each other again. I will not presume to tell you how to proceed in such a personal matter, beyond making one suggestion: Don't hold out the promise of continued friendship and future visits, unless you are very sure you can keep that promise. In theory, I can say it is better to keep the whole thing limited from the start by maintaining a sort of semi-business arrangement. If you see that one more session ought to clean things up, you can say something like, "I think I've got about another hour's worth of questions, so why don't I plan to come back once more next week for a sort of wrap-up?" I say "in theory," because that is much easier for me to suggest than it has been for me to do, and at the last moment I have blurted out, "Oh, I'll be back one of these days," when I was not at all sure I would be. The fact is, though, I have been lucky and made good on that promise more often than not. I have formed some lasting friendships through my field work. There are many towns in Maine and the Maritimes I wouldn't think of driving through without stopping to have a "shake-hands" with Edmund or Art or Jim or (as it happens more and more) driving out to the churchyard to stand a minute by their graves. As I say, I have been lucky. How you handle this problem is up to you, of course; just don't ignore it. And when you are through, write a thank-you letter.

Some Special Problems

The Recording of Music.   If I let myself panic into a full-scale treatise on it, the recording of music can sound like a pretty formidable and scary business. Therefore I am going to limit my remarks to the sort of field situation most users of this manual will be apt to find themselves in: recording someone singing or playing the fiddle in the parlor with the same basic middle-range equipment used for recording interviews. No doubt about it, music is much more difficult to handle than conversation, and a lot depends on how good your equipment is. It is amazing, for example, how much difference even a slightly better mike will make. Therefore, if you know ahead of time that the person you are going to interview is a singer or fiddle player and your main intention is to record his music, get the best equipment you can lay your hands on. If you are working out of an archives, perhaps you can get help there, or if you are working from a college or university base, you can check with the audiovisual center. However, the chances are you are going to have to use the equipment you already have. The first bit of advice I will offer, then, is not to let that fact worry you too much. Middle-range or even inexpensive equipment today is remarkably good.

As I have already suggested, it may be that you know ahead of time that your informant is a singer and are interviewing him for that reason. On the other hand, you may not know ahead of time. Say, for instance, you are interviewing an old woodsman, and in the course of things you ask him what men did in the evenings in camp. He mentions singing and you probe a bit: "What songs would they sing?" "Do you remember any of them?" If it looks as if he does remember some, especially if he gives some titles, ask him to sing one for you. Chances are there will be some initial resistance, and you will have to figure out whether he is really saying "*No*" or just wants to be coaxed a bit. Coaxing was and still is part of our musical tradition (would *you* sing at the first request, no matter how much you wanted to, or would you wait to be encouraged a bit? And would you not feel a bit disappointed if people took you at your word and didn't coax you?). No one can tell you how to coax someone, but I can offer two gimmicks that I have found useful.

First, get him to try, thus: "Look, I wish you'd just give it a try anyhow. Tell you what: let's record one song, and then you can listen to it. If you don't like what you hear, we just won't do any more, that's all." If this succeeds, I can only tell you that I have never had a man refuse to go on to more songs because he didn't like what he heard. Second, if he refuses to sing, ask him to *recite* the piece ("Well, could you just go over the words for me, just say it over?"). Then, after he has recited it, ask him to "just sing a couple of verses, so I can get the tune." On the basis of what you hear, you may be able to encourage him to sing the next song right through.

The line between the "no" that really means "yes" and the "no" that really means "no" is not always a clear one, but it is there. Never badger a man who clearly either cannot or will not sing, but remember that many people not only need to be coaxed, they *expect* to be. If he says no at one point in the interview, move on and come back to it later. And remember to try again next week.

If you launch into the whole matter of singing and songs, or (better yet) if he sings for you, spend some time talking about each song with him. Where did he learn it? Is it about something that really happened? How did he learn it? Did he ever know anyone who used to make up songs? Be especially inquisitive about local songs, the ones "made up by a fella around here."

You may have specific songs to ask for, and there is no reason why you should not, but it would also be interesting to see what songs the informant comes up with on his own. Try, that is, to get him to sing songs he likes, not songs you have asked for or that he thinks you might like. This can result in some interesting insights into taste, repertoire, and concept of categories. On that last point, you will find that while scholars and students talk of Child ballads, broadside ballads, or Native American ballads, singers speak of pirate songs, war songs, comical songs, ditties, etc. As a matter of fact, I have only heard the word "ballad" used twice in my life, both times to refer to printed copies of songs.

For technical hints on recording music, I would suggest reviewing the material on tape speed, microphones, and recording levels, but there are a few additional comments to be made. Be especially careful not to over-record. Sometimes I have asked a singer to give me a stanza or two so I could establish a good recording level, and it is a good plan, unless in your judgment it will make a singer who is already nervous feel just that much more "on stage," hence more nervous. If you would rather not go to this trouble, for whatever reason, simply turn the gain down (say from "one o'clock" to "twelve o'clock" or even a bit more) just before the informant starts to sing. Since a person usually sings louder than he talks, chances are that this will give you a workable level. Don't worry if your informant sings softly at first, especially if he is an older person who has not sung for a long time. That is a very common pattern.

As a rule, don't adjust the level while the song is going on. Of course, if the singer drives the needle into the red most of the time, cut the gain down right away. But that is an emergency measure. Simply avoid the strong temptation to fiddle with the gain during the song in order to get the perfect level. Wait until the song is over, then make an adjustment in anticipation of the next song. Since dynamics (louds and softs) are an important aspect of musical sound, any change in recording level during a performance will obscure them. For the same reason, by the way, never use automatic level control in recording music (unless you happen to have one of those machines that has nothing else, in which case you are stuck).

Using Photographs and Drawings.   Photographs, drawings, diagrams, and maps can add whole new dimensions to your interviews, or they can be an egregious waste of time. The difference is chiefly in how carefully and completely they are coordinated with and identified on the tape. That is, if a photograph is discussed during the interview, it must be clear which photograph it is, where the researcher can find it, and what within the photograph is being described. Actually this is simply one more application of the trialogue concept.

Three kinds of photographs are useful in interviews, and the same basic rules apply to all of them. First, there is the photograph you take yourself, of the informant, of the context, or of some object being discussed. It always helps someone listening to the tapes to have some idea of what the informant looks like; pictures of his home (both inside and out) and neighborhood may be even more helpful. While some interviewers spend almost as much time taking pictures as they do interviewing, others (myself for one) seldom bother with a camera at all, but there is no question in my mind that portrait and context photographs are valuable.

On the other hand, photographs of objects under discussion are often an absolute requirement. It is hard to imagine, for example, a successful interview about quilting that did not include clear photographs of patterns and techniques. Take your time with such photographs, and work out some system of identifying each one on the tape. If you take your pictures during the interview, you can simply say, "Wait, let me get a picture of that," and then add, "This is my picture number one." You may even pose the picture ("O.K. Show me just how you hold that knife now") or get the informant to point to some special feature you are discussing. You may find, though, that the camera gets in the way during the interview, in which case you can take your pictures all at once later on. If you choose this method, I suggest leaving the tape running during the photograph session. Your conversation about each picture and its specific details will thereby serve as a complete and numbered record of your photographs ("Would you hold up that log cabin quilt for me? Picture number four. . . . Fine. Now, how about pointing to that square you had so much trouble with? Picture number five. . . . "). Then follows an extremely important step: after your photographs are processed, you must not only work out a storage system that will make them easily available to the researcher, you must also coordinate the numbers you assign the photographs with those that appear in your catalog. More about that in a moment.

The second kind of photograph is the one you supply in order to elicit the informant's comments. Photographs can be great memory-joggers, but they have to be used carefully or they wind up creating horrendous frustrations. What are we to make of this little exchange, for example:

K: Can you tell me what this is in the picture?

P: Why sure, that's a water cart. Now, see, the rope would go up over there and out this way and then they'd hitch the horses on and they'd go out this way and the barrel'd come up full of water and. . . .

First of all, what picture? Where is the rope that went "over there?" (Where?) Which way was *this* way? The potential for confusion, here, is obvious. And even if *you* manage to understand what all this means, no one else will. So let me offer two simple rules.

Always identify each picture. For example, since each photograph in the Northeast Archives' files is numbered, all we have to do is give that number on the tape ("O.K., here's Archives photo 274. What's that. . . ."). If you use a photograph from a book, cite it clearly ("I've got a copy of Doerflinger's *Shantymen and Shantyboys* here, and there's a picture facing page 233 that I'd like to ask you about. . . ."). Then make sure that all the "this here's" and "that fella there's" and "this way's" are clarified. For example, the photograph so frustratingly described in the preceding paragraph is Northeast Archives photo number 29 (see below). If your informant (pointing) says the rope went "up over there," you can add, "You mean up over that triangular thing on the top of the box?" If he should identify one of the men ("Well what do you know! There's old Jack Furey. We used to. . . ."), you add "The one with his arms folded, right?" I have even found that it helps if I prepare questions about a photograph ahead of time, since in the heat of *his* describing what *he* sees, I frequently forget what it was that *I* wanted to know about the picture in the first place.

The third kind of photograph that is apt to become part of an interview is the one supplied by the informant. Say the interview is going along nicely, when suddenly the informant says, "I think I've got a picture of that right here" and produces a photograph album. The two rules (Identify and Describe) still hold, but you are going to have some trouble with the first one unless you can borrow the photograph for copying. If the informant is willing to let you do this (and that is the way it usually works out), get the work done and the photograph returned promptly. Your archives will probably have a copying service; if not, you may be able to locate a copier elsewhere. Either way, don't let borrowed material sit around too long. If the informant is unwilling to let you borrow the photograph, perhaps you can make arrangements to copy it on the spot (at the Northeast Archives, for example, we have a portable copy stand and camera for just this purpose).

Not every photograph the informant drags out is going to be worth copying, of course. You will have to make some judgments here, and sometimes you will not be able to tell immediately which photographs are valuable and which are not. I have spent a lot of time looking through piles of old photographs, while the tape was running, because there did not seem to be any alternative. Then I

Plate 1. Water-cart or road sprinkler for icing logging roads. (Photo reproduced by permission of the Northeast Archives of Folklore and Oral History)

would see one I wanted ("Hey, can I borrow that one to copy it? I'll get it back to you next week. O.K., we'll call this one number one. Now, what's this . . ."). On the other hand, sometimes, since it all seemed so irrelevant to my purposes but so relevant to the informant's, and since it looked like we were going to spend some time with the old album, I have shut the tape off (with some explanation such as "Look, I do want to look at these with you, so I'm just going to turn the machine off for a while.") Then take a few notes on photographs you do want and ask for them. Put a temporary identifying number on the back—lightly, and in pencil (felt tip pens can bleed through, and ball point or a pencil used with any force at all will permanently scar the print!). Later on, when you have started the tape again, you can go through the same process as described above ("I'm going to call this photograph number one. Now what did you say was going on here?"). These numbers will then go into your catalog, and when more permanent numbers are assigned to the photographs, you can simply add them in the proper place ("photo #3: NA 277"). Just remember not to cross out the temporary numbers, because they are still the numbers on the tape.

The same techniques should be used with maps or drawings, which will be taken from similar sources (your diagram, one from an outside source, or one prepared by the informant). I should offer one warning on maps, though: don't be surprised if your informant has no idea of how to read a map. I remember one old river-driver who knew every island in the Penobscot from Medway to Old Town, but when I showed him a map of the area, he could not figure it out at all. All his life he had seen those islands from the level of the water; a bird's-eye view meant nothing to him. Even if you have prepared maps at hand, it is frequently worth your while to ask the informant to draw his own (another one of the reasons why you bring plenty of paper and a pencil with you, always). You will be surprised what such maps can tell you about someone's sense of space (what is near and what far) and direction.

As a general rule, do not introduce photographs or drawings too soon. If possible, hold off on them until the second interview. If there will only be one interview, hold them until the latter stages of it. That is to say, don't *you* introduce them before that time. If your informant does, it's best to follow his lead and go along. But all too frequently interviewers bring out photographs before they are really ready for them. This is especially true of beginners, who may feel quite ill at ease and are only too glad to have something specific to talk about. Try not to panic into pictures. Take your time. You will do a better job for it, believe me.

While we are on the subject of visual materials, I should tell you what one man, Ernest Kennedy of Argyle, did for me. He wanted to make the operations of the Argyle Boom perfectly clear, and I arrived at his house one day to find that he had built a five-foot-long model of it! During the rest of the fall, as our interviews continued, he made models of an endways log raft, a driving dam complete with sluice, a batteau, a yard with a parbuckle, and a whole lumbercamp, all of which we spent parts of several interviews talking about, and all of which he gave to the Northeast Archives! That made the identity and description problem no different from what it would be with a drawing or a photograph, but knowing the mutability of things I am also filing a detailed batch of photographs carefully keyed to the interviews. Ernest's generosity deserves no less.

On-Site Interviewing. A man says, "Come on, hop in the car and I'll show you right where that was," or "I've got one of those out in the barn. Want to see it?" It sounds like a great idea, and it is, providing you keep in mind the same twin problems that exist for any "visual": identification and description. It may be necessary to include a careful map with your catalog, in order to make clear exactly where the informant took you, and you may find it helpful to "talk" the route right onto the tape as you move along ("We're heading down 178 toward Charlton. Now we're turning to the left three miles out of Wells, and there's a big white church on the corner . . .") Then you can retrace your path later, or you can check it on a state highway atlas or a "topo" map. Of course, if you expect to do much of this sort of thing, take some time in advance to learn what features the map is apt to show, then refer to them wherever you can.

Once you are on the site, the problem is the classical one of adequate description, along with some good probing, thus:

A: Now right here's where the old station used to be I was telling you about.

B: [*into mike*] We're about a hundred feet down the track to the left of where the old road crosses. [*To "A"*] Nothing much left to show it, is there, except for the clearing and all that crushed rock. How big a building was it?

Look hard for things to ask about ("What's that big iron drum over there?" . . . "Where did the road come to then?"). And of course, if you have a camera, use it: have the informant point to something, take a photograph, and record an explanation on the tape.

For most on-site interviews, it will probably pay you to come back later and do some more careful mapping. In this regard, I recommend learning how to take an accurate compass bearing. It is simple enough, and it is amazing what you can do with just a compass and a good steel tape (and a ruler, protractor, and pad of graph paper to record your results).

Speaking of maps, I have found one special kind of on-site interviewing very useful. I once wanted to get an idea of what a particular stretch of road was like seventy years ago, and I asked my informant if he would be willing to drive along that road with me and describe it as he remembered it. We started at the town line, where I set my trip odometer at zero, and then we talked our trip onto the tape something like this (my "asides" into the mike are indicated in italics):

Now right here there was a big farm-house (A: *1.4 miles on left.* How far back?) Oh seven or eight rods. That was the old Hawkins place. Charlie Hawkins was one of my oldest friends. (A: *1.7, crossing a brook.* Did this brook have a name?) No, never did that I knew. It usually dried up in August. Now right here's where Bob Coffin had that store I was telling you about (A: *2.1 on right.* Nothing there now.) No, his son moved it down the road to his place about twenty years ago. You can see it there now, that shed next to the barn (A: Oh, yeah. *Big white house, green trim, center gable, barn, shed. 2.6 on right.* What was his name?) Sterling. Sterling Coffin. Got killed in the war. Now over there. . . .

Almost certainly you will want to go over the route again by yourself, once you have made your "map," in order to check distances, add details of your own, and so forth. And before you set out with your informant, try recording by yourself in order to find the most workable level. Finally, I can only recommend this technique for back-country work, unless you have a friend do the driving (not a bad plan in any case). Try it on a busy village street and you will either have an accident or get a summons, or both. (Explain that one to the judge!)

Group Interviews. Any time you take on more than a single informant at once, you have a group interview. The group may be unexpected, as when you go to see a woman, and her husband is not only present but eager to talk too (Good luck to you on this one!). It may arise at the informant's suggestion ("My brother Floyd lives just two houses down, so I'll ask him to be here too. What I don't remember, maybe he will"). Or it may be your idea to bring two or three people of like interest together to see if they can "get each other going."

The inspiration for a group interview is usually honest enough. What folklorist has not found himself in a situation where half a dozen people are telling stories either in that time-honored natural context of enlightening the stranger or—and this less frequently—in that even more natural context of having cheerfully forgotten the stranger was there. And the folklorist sits silently, the hair on the back of his neck rising with his pulse rate, and thinks, "Oh, if I only had my tape recorder here *now*!" I remember saying that once while driving round trip from Newcastle to Sackville, New Brunswick, with two fine singers and a bottle of Lamb's Navy Rum. My two friends roared out song after song, telling great stories in between. Yet deep down I knew that if I had the tape recorder there, it would not be the same at all (unless I had "sneaked it," and I have already made my attitude on that kind of shabbiness perfectly clear).

In all cases, the group interview raises special problems which, while not unsolvable, can be exasperating. First of all, there are the technical problems like where to place the mike to pick up both voices, and if there are more than two the problem gets geometrically worse. Cataloging and transcription are made at least equally more difficult, as you try to identify voices or separate out what two people are saying at once. But problems of this order should not turn you against the technique, for it not only may work, it may work splendidly. The real problem that often spoils group interviews is quite simple: one person dominates, and it is not always the person who really knows the most. This self-appointed spokesman will interrupt, talk over, and even contradict the others to the point where they volunteer less and less, even though you try to draw them out. In other words, you wind up, in effect, with a one-on-one interview anyhow, only with the wrong informant. If you are skillful enough to handle this sort of situation, fine; you may even create a more natural context than would be possible in a one-on-one interview. I never have had much luck with it, though, which may in part explain my preference for one-on-one interviews in the first place.

I have sometimes found a group interview useful for a start, a first interview which I can follow up with individual interviews ("Look, the other day when I asked how Breakneck Hill got its name you started to talk when Harry cut you off. What were you going to say?"). Listen closely to the tape of that group interview, and you will find all kinds of leads and clues, but in the end, the burden of the work for tape-recorded interviews will be one-on-one.

More Than One Interviewer, Or "Taking a Friend."   Many interviewers feel the need for a companion, especially when they are going for their first interview with a total stranger. It is hard to recommend against anything that makes ice-breaking a little easier, and therefore I will not advise against it, even though I see the straight one-on-one situation as basic. The presence of a second interviewer is not so much a *bad* idea as it is the cause of special problems you ought to keep in mind both before deciding to invite someone else and, once you have so decided, during the interview itself.

Obviously it will make a difference *whom* you take. Sometimes the person who recommended the informant will volunteer to go along, and that may sound innocent enough, but it can happen that the informant will spend most of the interview talking to the old friend, not to you. Such an arrangement may be worth your time, though, just for the entrée; you can always go back again. Sometimes, though, the volunteer local "broker" can put you in a bind. I remember one woman up in New Brunswick who offered to take me around and introduce me to some great singers she knew, and the results were nearly disastrous. Not only did she turn out to be just the wrong person (though as an outsider I had no way of knowing that), but since all the real singers in that culture were men, my introduction by a woman was hardly to be taken seriously. It may, of course, be all but impossible to refuse this sort of help, and perhaps the best advice that I can give is that you accept it—it could be great! —but keep an eye to leeward.

The man/woman relationship will be important too. If you are a girl and you take your boyfriend with you to interview a man, if you are a boy and you take a girl with you to interview an old railroad worker, if you are a girl and take a boy to interview a farm wife, or if you are married and take your wife or your husband along, it *will* make a difference. But there is no need to assume that that difference will be negative or restrictive. In fact it is very interesting, in any such situation to notice who captures the informant's attention. One girl told me that even though she was "officially" the interviewer and asked all the questions, the man she was interviewing directed every answer to her boyfriend. On the other hand, I remember one time when I took one of my female students with me to interview an old river-driver, and while he directed his answers to me, for the most part, he answered *her* questions in more detail than he did mine. It is impossible to predict what difference the presence of a companion of the opposite sex will make in your interview, but the difference can tell you a lot. Again, don't be afraid of it; just be alert to it.

One special problem (especially, I have found, in husband/wife visits) occurs when the informant's spouse is also present: two conversations get going at once, the husband talking to the man, the wife talking to the woman. This situation usually arises out of the informant couple's desire to be hospitable, but it does not always remain hospitable. I have seen men obviously annoyed when their wives kept "butting in" or "going on," even though they were "going on" to my wife, and I have known men who have become very restive and noisy when I showed much interest in what their wives might be saying to my wife. For the purpose of collecting folklore, these "double interviews" can be very fruitful, but on tape they can be chaos. One of the simplest solutions to this kind of crosstalk is to try to split the two pairs; the interviewer's wife, for example, might show interest in something in the kitchen and thereby move her conversation out there.

The age of your companion can make an important difference too, and I will close this section with an example. One girl wanted to interview an elderly woodsman, and since her uncle had worked in the woods she thought it would be a good plan to take him along. The two men did not know each other, but they soon discovered what a lovely time they could have teasing her by sharing all kinds of silent understandings. As she asked questions, the informant would give cryptic answers and then wink at the uncle, whereupon they would both chuckle. This went on for over an hour, while she grew more and more frustrated and angry. When she told me about it, two days later, she was still steaming. "What I really wanted to do," she said, "was decapitate the two of them with a rusty crosscut saw I'd seen in the shed!" If she had, before any jury of her true peers she would certainly have been acquitted.

Obtaining a Release

A release is simply a signed statement by the informant that he understands the terms under which the interview took place and is willing for it to be used according to those terms. Most archives require releases and have their own forms which you will be requested to use, but even if you are working independently you should consider getting some form of release. Samples of Northeast Archives releases are printed in the Appendix, and you may wish to model yours on them, but there are as many forms of releases as there are archives.

Many interviewers find it hard to ask for a release, feeling that it is an imposition or even an impertinence. I know I hated to ask at first, but as time went on and neither I nor my students encountered any refusals, I found it bothering me less and less. Now it is routine, though still a part of the routine I wish I could dispense with. But I will not, and you should not. After all, you will mention it in your explanation at the beginning of the interview, and if there are going to be any objections, they should surface at that time. But very seldom will there be any objections at all. Just wait and see.

When should you get the release signed? I used to suggest getting it at the end of the entire series of interviews, but it too often happened that I would plan to get back for more interviews with someone and for any of a number of reasons never did, which meant that

I would have interviews for which there were no releases at all. On the strength, then, of my own experience, I suggest getting a release *at the end of every interview*. Of course, that may mean you will have half a dozen releases from the same person, but that is no problem. An interview for which you have no release *is* a problem— if not for you, at least for your archives.

Most informants will accept and sign a reasonable release without hesitation, but for some reason, your informant may have reservations or wish to restrict access to or use of the interview. That is, of course, his right. Both of you "own" the interview equally, since it was your joint creation, and both of you must be satisfied as to its disposition. There may be good reason why the material in the interview should be restricted, and if, after talking it over with your informant, you feel his reservations are reasonable, see what sort of restrictions he wants to impose. Work it out with him, but if you feel his demands are excessive, you will have to decide whether or not to go ahead with the interview. I mentioned above that since the interview is the joint creation of you and your informant, both of you have equal rights in it. Your archives, therefore, will probably ask you to sign a release too (see the Northeast Archives form in the Appendix), and you may have your own restrictions to impose. If you are working on a book, for instance, it would be perfectly reasonable for you to ask that no one else be permitted to publish material from your interviews for five or even ten years, until you have had a chance to do something with it yourself. But don't be a dog in the manger. In the world of scholarship, the more open things can be, the better for us all.

A Final Word on Interviewing

This chapter has been replete, resplendent, and (who knows) maybe even refulgent with suggestions on how to conduct interviews, all of it good advice, and all of it derived from years of experience. But there is one last thing that will be a comfort to remember: just as there is no such thing as the perfect marriage, or the perfect crime, or even the perfect rose, there is no such thing as the perfect interview. You will never listen to a tape of one of your own interviews and not be at least a little dismayed at your blunders ("Why didn't I ask. . . ." "Boy was that ever a dumb question. . . ." "I shoulda followed that up. . . ." etc.). I have never had an interview in which I translated every "over here" or "about this long" the way I know I should, and some of the photo descriptions I have elicited are, sad to say, useless jumbles of "this-heres" and "hims." But in spite of my acknowledged foot of clay, I have been shambling down the road for better than twenty years, and in that time I have done some pretty good interviews—some of them, if I may say so, remarkable. My final bit of advice is to get on with it, then. It is all right to be dismayed at your blunderings, so long as you accept them as inevitable and go ahead. It's a good road to travel.

3. Processing

The Primary Document

That was the exciting part: going out and interviewing someone. What follows is far from exciting: making the resultant tape a useful and usable primary research document. That takes time and careful, systematic work, but if you skimp on it, you might just as well have stayed home in the first place. There are many different approaches to this processing, and while I will go into most detail on the way we do the work at the Northeast Archives, I will try to give enough information about other approaches to make an intelligent choice among them possible. But since the approach you choose will depend heavily on what you decide is the primary document, we should spend a little time defining that term.

A primary document is one behind which there is nothing. A letter or a diary, for example, would be a primary document, while versions of them reproduced in a book—no matter how carefully done—would be secondary documents. By analogy, then, it would appear that the tape recording should be looked on as the primary document and any transcription of it considered secondary.[11] While that is essentially how I conceive of them, there are two important qualifications, one theoretical and one practical, that I would like to make.

In theory, the tape recording is still a secondary document, because *the interview itself* is primary, the tape being no more than the best available record of that interview. But since there is no way yet available of returning to the interview itself, the point is moot. On the other hand, if what you do is to transcribe the interview and then send the transcription to the informant for correction or amplification, and if the informant does in fact make alterations—deleting passages, adding fuller explanations, correcting sentence structure,

11. For an interesting working-out of this problem as it applies to linguistic geography—and one that has important implications for folklore and oral history—see Lee Pederson, "Tape/Text and Analogues," *American Speech,* 49 (Spring–Summer, 1974), pp. 5–23.

and the like—then the resultant manuscript becomes the primary document, the tape and transcript merely rough drafts. In this situation, if you want to find out what the informant "said" about something, you would not go to the tape but to the corrected transcript.

As a general rule, oral history archives have emphasized the importance of the final transcript, and while the tapes are usually retained in some fashion, they are very seldom referred to. Folklore archives have generally taken the opposite approach; not only is the tape the working document, there are often no complete transcriptions, and even the catalogs may offer only a bare outline of the tape's content. At the Northeast Archives of Folklore and Oral History, we have tried to take a middle ground. While we consider the tape the primary document, we encourage transcription and insist on rather complete catalogs as an absolute minimum requirement. Yet the purpose of these secondary documents is essentially to facilitate finding material on the tape, and in no sense are they considered an adequate substitute for it. In short, we do everything we can to persuade the researcher to listen to the tape and make his own transcription of relevant material rather than to depend upon someone else's transcript.

There should be no question about it, though: a transcript is a very nice thing to have. It is by far the best record of what is on the tape, calling attention to items that are far too brief or peripheral to appear in any catalog. But transcripts present two big problems. First, as I have already suggested, they tend to become ends in themselves, usurping the rightful place of the tape as primary document. Second, they are very expensive and time-consuming, taking anywhere from ten to twenty hours, per hour of interview, to produce. In contrast, we find that it takes about three to five hours per interview-hour to produce a good catalog according to our specifications. It comes to this: if you have the time or the money, you can opt for complete transcripts. If you do not, you can try our solution. It is working very well for us.

The Complete Catalog

You should make your catalog just as soon after the interview as you can, ideally when you get home that evening. If you wait, you will forget things like proper names or what that funny noise was. At the very least, you should prepare your catalog before you go back for another interview. In this way you will have a good review of what went on, what was covered, what remains to be covered, what needs clarification, and so on. Never delay, then; get to the catalog right away.

While you are working on the catalog, keep a pad of paper handy for jotting down questions you will want to ask, and *jot a question down the minute you think of it.* Believe me, that statement is important enough for italics. Don't "make a mental note" to jot it down as soon as you "finish this sentence," and by no means count on a review of the completed catalog to suggest questions. By that time you will have forgotten, and the catalog will seem smooth enough to make it appear that everything was perfectly clear. Keep that pad right at hand, and take a moment to write your questions out clearly ("Jam-breaking with dynamite. Here he says they placed the charge 'a ways back' from the face. Earlier he said *at* the face. Which?" Rather than "dynamite: where placed?"). You will be surprised how cryptic the latter question can appear even a few hours later.

The catalog is an extremely important document for two reasons. First, it is the only available description of what is on the tape (and in the Northeast Archives, it will be the basis for any indexing work we will do). Even if time and money do become available at some date in the future to allow for a complete transcription, the catalog will be all you have in the meantime. But let us assume for the moment that the lucky day comes around when the tape can be transcribed. Then, whoever does the work will be utterly dependent on the catalog for the spelling of proper names, the names of tools and processes, the explanation of interruptions, extra voices, noises, and other such matters. Thus, a little extra care in making the catalog will save others hours of work later on, be those others researchers or transcribers.

First of all, then, if you are using the Northeast Archives catalog form (see the sample catalog in the Appendix), fill in the material at the top of the first page completely. Get complete addresses, for instance, so that we could get in touch with either you or the informant if we had to. Even if you are not using the Northeast Archives form, you should make sure that the information it covers is available. Your "Brief Description of Contents" should be brief, but it should be long enough to give anyone reading it a clear idea of what sort of material the interview involved. "Talk with Mrs. Ledbetter about old times" is not enough, for example. *What* did Mrs. Ledbetter talk about?

Reminder: Never use battery power for cataloging work!

Make the catalog not for yourself (as something to remind *you* of the tape's contents) but for someone who has never heard the tape before. Try, as you listen to the tape, to anticipate all the problems a scholar or transcriber might have with it, and resolve them ahead of time by explaining them in the catalog. One of the things that means is spelling out all proper names, place names, and the like. This will be a hard rule to follow sometimes, because surely everyone knows how to spell, say, "Smith" (sure: "S-m-y-t-h-e"). There will be spellings you won't get; that's bound to happen. All right, there's a question to be asked next time ("What was the name of that river where you almost got drowned?"). You may have to do some map work yourself, but under any circumstances you should look on the clarification and spelling of proper names and terms of the trade ("peavey," "pot warp," etc.) as part of *your* responsibility.

Write your catalog as a rather detailed summary of what is on the tape—a complete précis. It is of course possible for a catalog to be too complete and detailed, but it is more common for people to leave out essential material. One of the most common kinds of omission occurs when the interviewer/cataloger makes judgments about what is or is not "relevant." Say you are interviewing a woman about her experiences as a telephone operator, and she veers off into a discussion of what is wrong with the educational system today. Don't leave that out of your catalog, and don't slight it with something like "Mrs. Harter digresses on schools." Like it or not, that material is on the tape, and, on the chance that it may be useful to someone someday, you should summarize her opinions on this matter along with everything else. Just as the tape should be as accurate a record as possible of what went on in the interview, the catalog should be an accurate description of what is on the tape. In your capacity as cataloger, never get involved in value judgements. There will be time enough for that later on.

One of the rules of good summary writing is to avoid direct quotation of the original. Basically, it is a good rule, but I frequently find some phrase or sentence that serves my summarizing purpose at least as well as my own words would. Under such circumstances, there is no reason why you should not use direct quotation occasionally, but always indicate what you are doing by placing such words in quotation marks.

Perhaps the best general cataloging advice I can give is to tell you to avoid "how" entries. "How they built boom piers" tells us very little. Put down a summary of what the informant said ("They built boom piers in the wintertime on the ice, first laying down a solid bed of logs, then. . . ."). In other words, *describe*; don't simply *indicate* what is there. It helps to write in complete sentences, but that is not absolutely necessary. Just stay away from cryptic little phrases that may mean something to you but will mean nothing to anyone else later on ("The success bit again". . . "Charlie Roberts' deadfall").

In what "person" should you cast the catalog? I have found that casting the whole thing in first person is by far the simplest and most economical method. That is, say "I left school after I got in a fight with my teacher," rather than "He left" or worse yet, "Mr. Franco left." Using the first person will also allow you to keep the informant's use of pronouns rather than having to make awkward translations ("I told him that he . . ." rather than "He told him that he . . ."), and it will help you avoid such useless fillers as "Mr. Franco explains that . . ." Occasionally you may wish to include one of your questions in the summary, in which case you can use third person for yourself thus: "EDI asks where he met his wife." A tape is in the first person, and a transcript would be, so why not the catalog as well?

As you work on your catalog, there will be phrases and words that are unclear. If you are fairly certain of what you hear, it will not hurt to include the word with a question mark after it, thus: "Maynard(?)." But if you find yourself really stumped, leave a blank that is *longer* than the word or phrase in question and go ahead, making a note on your question pad to ask about it next time. Sometimes you may be pretty sure of what was said but not sure enough to type it in, in which case you might write it in the blank space in pencil. Later on, if you find out what the word or name was, you can fill it in permanently, but if you don't find out, a blank (with or without something tentatively penciled in) is far better than a wild guess.

A number of circumstances will call for the inclusion of material that is not on the tape. All such material should be enclosed in brackets and underlined. You should explain all extraneous noises [clock strikes], account for all breaks [Tape turned off for five minutes while she goes to look for photograph album], identify all photographs [looking at photo #11], and add anything you think will make listening to the tape more meaningful [His wife was shaking her head "no" to me from the kitchen door as he said this]. One minor exception to this procedure is in the matter of gestures of distance and position that you did not get onto the tape. If the informant said something was "about that long," and you remember his gesture, you can record the information directly in the catalog as "about three feet long."

I should add a word on paragraphing. Keeping in mind that the catalog is intended to help people find material on the tape easily, break paragraphs wherever a break seems to make sense, avoiding page-long paragraphs on the one hand, one-sentence paragraphs on the other. You will have to make your own decisions here, but I think you will find that the nature of your material will help you make them intelligently.

How long should your catalog be? I have one interview of about two hours for which the catalog runs (on Northeast Archives forms) to twenty pages (the complete transcript is over seventy); in another, an hour's interview runs to sixteen pages (while the transcript runs to forty). Some interviews are less "packed" than others, and much will depend on how easy a talker your informant is. Generally, nine to fifteen double-spaced pages per hour of interview appears to be about right. Some interviews will go more than that, and conceivably some could go less. But there, at least, are some guidelines.

As has already been pointed out, the digital counters found on tape recorders are far from standardized; not only do they vary from one make to another, but different machines of the same make will vary somewhat too. In spite of these variations, we at the Northeast Archives have found that tape catalogs keyed to these counters have worked very well, so long as field workers follow a few simple rules and procedures to maintain as much standardization as possible. First, when you put the tape on your machine to begin cataloging, take two or three winds around the spindle of the take-up reel in order to seat the tape firmly. Then set the digital counter at 000, and advance by "fast forward" to where the interview begins (at about 020). In other words, the digital counter should be set at 000 at the beginning of the *tape,* not at the beginning of the *interview.* From here on in, cite counter numbers in the catalog wherever it seems logical to do so, but in general don't space them out too far; they will be most useful at intervals of two or three citations per 100 digits.

If you come to the end of the interview on side one, put "END OF INTERVIEW" in your catalog, indicating the counter number at which the interview ends, and rewind the tape onto the original (i.e. supply) reel. If, however, the interview is continued on side two, put "END OF SIDE ONE" and the counter number in your catalog and go "fast forward" to the end. Turn the tape over, re-thread it (again taking two or three winds to seat the tape firmly), *reset the digital counter to 000,* put "BEGINNING OF SIDE TWO" in your catalog, and start cataloging again.

The sample catalog in the Appendix should give you a good idea of how we at the Northeast Archives handle this calibration. Notice, for instance, that we have two calibration columns and that the interviewer enters his calibrations in the one marked "Int." Later, as part of the basic accessioning process, we will mark off our own calibrations every hundred digits on one of our office machines (notice too that a record is made of what machine was used to work out each set of digits). It is not a perfect system, but we have found that by having both sets of calibrations, and doing a little interpolating, we can find any segment of the tape we need quite efficiently. Thus, the best recommendation I can make for our system is that it works.[12]

12. Dale Treleven and his colleagues at The State Historical Society of Wisconsin have worked out a very interesting indexing technique involving a two-track stereo system with the recorded interview on one track and a recorded time-signal on the other, which, when keyed to a catalog, seems to allow for very efficient location of specific items on the tape. Anyone interested in the details (called the Wisconsin TAPE System) should write Mr. Treleven, c/o State Historical Society of Wisconsin, 816 State Street, Madison, Wisconsin 53706.

Making A Transcript

At some point, it will be necessary to make a transcription of parts of the interview for use in research or writing. However, most oral history archives require *complete* transcriptions, and, as I have already pointed out, a transcript is a very nice thing to have. If you decide to make a complete transcript, it will not be necessary for you to make a complete catalog of the type described above. A transcript made in the manner described on the following pages will more than suffice as a description of the tape's contents.

In preparing to transcribe, one of the first things you should decide is the level of accuracy at which you intend to work. This decision will be largely dictated by the purpose the material will serve in your research. A dialectician will be concerned with pronunciation; a historian probably will not be. A psychologist doing pausal analysis will be interested in the length of every pause and the exact number and location of every "uh" and "er"; a folklorist might not require this kind of detail at all. The archives or program for which you are working may have requirements of its own, of course, which you will have to accept. What follows are the instructions we at the Northeast Archives give to people doing their own transcriptions for deposit with us. They strike a kind of middle level of accuracy that we have found adequate for most purposes, since the assumption can be made that the tape is easily available to anyone requiring more detail.

Remember too that we consider the tape the primary document, the ultimate authority. A transcript of any sort is simply the best representation you can make of what is on the tape, but since it *is* a representation, it is unavoidably an interpretation. No two people will transcribe the same tape in exactly the same way, even if they are following the same set of guidelines, nor will the same person transcribe it in the same way on two different occasions (try it and see). We must accept this sort of variation as inherent in the whole process, but accepting it as a limitation in no way invalidates the process itself. Rather, the process is strengthened, because we will use it more intelligently, knowing as we do what can reasonably be expected of it.

Always use a good quality paper, something that will stand handling, preferably "non-acidic" or "pH neutral" for longer shelf life. Avoid "erasable bonds," since they have a tendency to smear with handling. Double-space everything, and leave good one-inch margins at left, top and bottom, and at least half an inch on the right. Corrections may be inked in (black ink only), so long as you print neatly and clearly. Crossing-out is permitted, and so is erasing and the use of white-out correction tape or fluid, so long as the page remains completely legible. Of course, if it gets messed-up pretty badly (say to the point where it might not make a clear photocopy), it should be rewritten, but accuracy and readability are more important than neatness for its own sake. Beautiful is nice, but accurate and readable is better, while beautiful, accurate, and readable is best of all.

At the top of the first page of your transcription, set down essentially the same information you find in your opening announcement, thus: "Northeast Archives of Folklore and Oral History. Accession number 765, tape number 765.1. Interview by Thurlow Blankenship with John O'Connor, Edinburg, Maine, September 28, 1978." Following that, if you have used initials to identify the different speakers in the body of the interview, give their full names, thus: "B = Thurlow Blankenship, O = John O'Connor."

Now begin the transcription proper, using dialogue form, thus:

K: Did you ever have any uh close shaves?

J: Close shaves? You mean like was I, did I almost ever get myself killed? Well, only once that I can recall, but that was enough. [laughs]

K: What happened that time?

J: You want to hear about that, do you? All right, *etc.*

For all material not actually on the tape, follow the same format you would use if you were making a complete catalog: enclose it in brackets and underline it. You may want to explain an extraneous sound [loud bang at this point: caused by cow exploding outside the window], or describe a gesture [demonstrating: clasps hands over head]. Or you may wish to indicate that the informant directed a remark to someone else [calls to wife in kitchen]. One of the most important functions of such "stage directions" is to explain why certain passages are unintelligible. It may be that something went wrong with the tape recorder or that the informant's granddaughter came into the room and turned the television set on, drowning out the interview. In all such cases, your note should be full enough to really explain what happened:

> B: What did you use for that?
> J: Well, you'd use a crimper. I think I've got one right here in this [at this point, Mrs. Jones started looking through a lot of utensils in a drawer in the table we were sitting at, and the noise makes it impossible to hear what she is saying for about ten seconds] used to be right in there. Well, anyway, *etc.* . . .

Even under the most ideal circumstances, though, there will inevitably be words, phrases, and even longer passages that you simply will not be able to understand, in spite of the fact that you conducted the interview yourself. The Northeast Archives rule-of-thumb here is to listen three times, then move on, leaving a blank that is at least as long as—and preferably longer than—the unintelligible passage. As I have recommended elsewhere, if you *think* you know what was said, or if you hear what is said but it just does not make any sense to you, leave a blank, but write in your tentative interpretation *in pencil.* You will clarify a lot of this material as you review your transcript by going through the tape a second time, or some future listener will be able to make it out. This possibility prompts a final suggestion: get a friend to listen to the puzzling passage; it is amazing how often all that is required is a fresh pair of ears! Failing that, though, three times and move on is a good working rule. Thus, in places, your transcript might look something like this:

> K: We'd come downstream as far as where
>   Brook comes in and Charlie
> hollered to me to
>   or I'd get myself killed. So I
> reached out, *etc.*

There may be times when a blank space will run for the equivalent of several sentences, or even a whole paragraph. No matter, leave plenty of room.

Inevitably comes the question: must everything be transcribed? The answer is yes, but a qualified yes: *transcribe everything in ac-*

cordance with the level of accuracy at which you or your archives intend to work. At the Northeast Archives, we used to insist on the transcription of all "uh's," all backing-and-filling, all false starts, and all tag questions ("you see?" or "know what I mean?"). We no longer require such detail, partly because we found it practically impossible to transcribe consistently (some "uh's" and "y'knows" were always left out) and partly because of our conviction that the tape is the primary document and anyone requiring that level of accuracy would be a fool to trust someone else's transcriptions. For example, someone following our old instructions would have had to transcribe a passage as follows:

> K: Did you ever work on, well, on other rivers besides the Penobscot?
>
> J: Did I what uh, did I uh well, let me think uh yeah now sure yeah sure I uh drove the uh uh the Kennebec River one no it was one spring yes.

We would now suggest that passage be transcribed this way:

> K: Did you ever work on other rivers besides the Penobscot?
> J: Well, let me think. Yeah, I drove the Kennebec River one spring.

The passage may be a bit extreme to begin with, but not all that extreme: you will get many like it. If you do have an informant who responds in this halting manner, it is a good plan to say something about it in a headnote to the transcription:

> [Note: Mr. King's speech is so full of hesitations, haltings, false starts, and tag questions that occasionally I have had to exercise some judgement in deciding what to put in, what to leave out.]

Usually, though, such omissions can be taken for granted.

Another omission we have decided to permit is interviewer interjections. We used to insist on their inclusion, enclosing them in parentheses in order not to break up the narrative flow, thus:

> B: We were coming down that hill just beyond Lily Bay there (I: uh-huh), and the road was just a little slick. It had rained the night before, see (I: yeah), and it was still a little cold that early in the morning, know what I mean? (I: oh, sure) Well, *etc.*

Once again, we feel that someone interested in such supportive devices should be working directly from tape. However, if you decide you want to include them, our old system works very well.

Sometimes a pause can be as significant as anything that is said, maybe significant enough to be in the transcription. There is no hard and fast rule here; you will have to exercise some judgement as to whether a pause is meaningful or just part of the informant's speech pattern. It may, for example, be significant that the informant hesitates for some time before he answers a question, if you have determined that he *normally* does not do that. Indicate such important pauses by giving their approximate length:

> J: We were stuck out there on that little center jam and the water was rising and we was in one hell of a fix I tell you. Then a man by the name of—oh, what was his name? [pause: 5 sec.] Well, it don't matter none now, but he *etc.*

How about dialect? There are strong differences of opinion as to whether one should try to represent pronunciation by altering spellings, but we at the Northeast Archives strongly recommend that you stay away from any representation of dialect in transcripts. Don't write "wa'p" when you know the informant would probably spell it "warp" for example, or "jest" for "just," and don't leave off final "g's" (write "going," not "goin' "). Transcribed dialect always contains within it an element of condescension, and you will never have to apologize for or "explain" the use of standard spelling. And for Heaven's sake, keep away from eye dialect ("wuz" for "was"). Dialect is important, but a transcription should not be made to bear the burden of it. Once again, if a researcher is interested in this level of detail, he should be working with the tapes, and your transcription can show him just where on the tapes to look.

Given these exceptions—tags, interjections, false starts, dialect— the basic rule is still valid: Get everything down that is on the tape. Don't record what you think the informant *meant* to say; put down exactly what he did say, without "correcting" grammar, usage, or sentence structure. Nine times out of ten it will be perfectly clear how you should handle a passage, but you will inevitably have to make some decisions. Take the following passage, for example:

> J: I don't know, I don't know that I ever had a a tougher job a tougher job handed me. But the uh the uh two of us, him and me, him and me together, we—on that unjeezily job, all winter we was man and man about.

I would be inclined to transcribe the passage as follows:

> J: I don't know that I ever had a tougher job handed me. But the two of us, him and me together on that unjeezily job, all winter we was man and man about.

This preserves the informant's grammar, word order, and usage (a word like "unjeezily" is a word, but you will have to decide how such words should be spelled). I would consider the following version as taking too many liberties:

> J: I don't know that I was ever given a tougher job, but he and I worked man and man about on it all winter.

How do you handle two people talking at once? One of the best ways I know is to separate the two speeches to the best of your ability, then connect them with a brace in the margin, thus:

> J: Did the fire ever get this close to town?
> { Mr.: Oh goodness, yes, it burned Herman Jones'—
> { Mrs.: No, I don't think that fire ever did. He's thinking about the 1948 fire. Now that one, *etc.*

The brace would indicate that both Mr. and Mrs. were talking at once, while the dashes would indicate that he broke off while she continued. If the confusion is too great for this convenient device to bear, you may simply have to explain in a stage direction: [Mr. and Mrs. Smith were both talking together here, and it is very hard to tell what's going on, but the gist is that he felt it had while she was sure it hadn't].

As I have said already, no two people will transcribe a passage in exactly the same way. That variation from transcriber to transcriber will be nowhere more evident than in the matter of punctuation; one person will use a period where another person will use a comma. Punctuation marks (Victor Borge to the contrary notwithstanding) are conventions of print, and in making a transcription you will adapt them to represent the conventions of spoken language (pauses, alterations of pitch and loudness, and the like), which means once again you will have to make judgments. Work them out as best you can. Usually you can "feel" sentences clearly enough, and that can tell you where to put your periods and question marks. And since a lot of people begin sentences with conjunctions, don't feel compelled to comma a speech into one vast run-on sentence in obedience to a school-teacher rule that says you must not begin a sentence with a conjunction (a silly rule, almost as silly as the one that says a preposition is something you shouldn't end a sentence with). If the informant drops his voice and pauses in a way that tells you *that* sentence is over, put a period. Two hyphens (--) can be used to show where an informant breaks off or was interrupted. Work out the rest of the text with commas and semicolons. Use exclamation points sparingly, and the same can be said of underscoring for emphasis. There is only one absolute prohibition: don't use a series of spaced periods to indicate anything in a transcription. These are standard ellipsis marks, indicating that something has been left out, three (. . .) indicating less than a sentence, four (. . . .) indicating more than a sentence. They will have their place when a researcher quotes a passage from a tape or transcription in his published work, but their inclusion in a transcript could be confusing. Any omissions in a transcript (and as a rule there should be none) should be fully explained, both as to content and extent, in brackets and underlined.

In order that the transcript be as useful and convenient as possible for finding material on the tape, you should cite digital counter calibrations every so often—about as often as you would if you were making a complete catalog. But in the catalog you put them in the margin in a special column; in a transcript, put them in the body of the text and circle them in black thus:

> R: We'd go across the river on the logs, thousands and thousands, all full of spruce gum. And we'd pick chunks of spruce gum and we'd come down and sell it to Burnham Drug Company. ⓪435 Somedays we'd go fishing too, *etc.*

Be sure to indicate what machine (make, model, and even the specific machine, if possible) you used for the calibrations. Following your transcript, and using your calibrations, any researcher will find it relatively easy to locate the desired passage on the tape. And that is what we want to encourage him to do!

How do you transcribe songs or poems? Begin with an indication such as [sings:] or [recites:]. Then listen to the whole song or poem and try to "fetch out" the lengths of lines and the stanza structure. It is not as hard or as arcane a task as it might seem. Most people, including almost all of those who claim they are "tone deaf" (which they really aren't), can handle it by listening for pauses—short at the ends of lines, longer at the ends of stanzas—and the places where the tune seems to "break some" (at the end of a line), "come to an end," or "start over" (at the end of a stanza). Try it a few times. Then get a friend to try it, or compare the stanza form you fetched out with what someone else may have used in publishing that song in a collection. The following is a good example of how your transcript should look:

> I: I was wondering if you ever heard a song called "The West Branch" or some call it "John Roberts."
> K: Yes, sure, I've heard it, and I think I even know it all. Let's see, how did that begin now [pause: 10 sec.] Yeah. O.K. now [sings:]
> John Roberts as I understand
> He was a brave and fine young man
> He hired out with Mr. Brown
> To help him bring his lumber down.
>
> Up the West Branch he then did go
> It proved his [pause: 5 sec.] proved his sad overthrow
> He ventured out to break a jam
> And fell beneath the rolling dam.

Ultimately, the tune should be transcribed too, but that is a whole new subject involving special skills, techniques, and (hopefully) training. Unless you are such a specialist, just keep a good record, both in your catalog and in the transcript, of where the tunes are that will need transcription.

I have already alluded several times to the fact that you should always make a final check of your transcript by listening to the tape once more and following it through on the transcript. This second check is very important. Not only is it possible that you will find things you neglected to transcribe the first time (it does not happen often, but it happens), you will also find that many unintelligible things will suddenly become perfectly clear. These additions and corrections should be either typed in or *printed in black pen* (blue pen and script often show up poorly in photocopies).

Should the transcript be shown to the informant or sent to him for correction? That is one of the basic procedures for oral history programs, and while we at the Northeast Archives always allow the informant this privilege if he requests it, it is not part of our normal processing. The informant's release reminds the user that he is "reading a transcript of my spoken, not my written word, and that the tape, not the transcript, is the primary document." We consider the transcript completed when the interviewer checks it for the last time. But under any circumstances, if the informant requests permission to check the transcript—or even to correct it—that settles it: it is his right. We would send him a photocopy and, when he returned it, file both the original and corrected copy (unless, of course, we were asked to do otherwise).[13]

Final Disposition and Future Use

At the beginning of the first chapter, the research method described in this book was said to consist of two separate but interrelated activities: first, the holding of extended, taped interviews, and, second, the processing of those interviews so that their contents will be easily available to both yourself and others. We have now covered the field work proper and as much of the processing as would usually be carried out by the interviewer. From this point on, the materials are handled by the archives, but as a field worker you should know how the material is further processed once it leaves your hands. The problem is that every archives will have its own system, and while it is no part of the plan of this book to recommend our system at Northeast Archives over any others—or even to discuss

13. Although there is no question but that the interviewer is the person best qualified to make the transcriptions, there are commercial transcription services available. Two that come to mind are Tapes Into Type, c/o Oral History Program, L-243, California State University, Fullerton, Calif. 92634; and Bureau of Office Services, 3935 North Pulaski Road, Chicago, Illinois 60641.

archiving in any detail—our system is enough like others to allow it to serve as an example.

When someone brings in a tape with its catalog or transcript, we assign both an accession number. Our numbers run serially from the first collection we received to the most recent, but many archives assign numbers by year (that is, 78-14 for the fourteenth accession in 1978). It makes little difference what system is used, so long as it is consistent and the same number is placed on both the tape (we mark it on the reel with indelible felt-tip pen) and the accompanying paperwork. We also record an announcement on the beginning of the tape (having instructed all our field workers to leave the first twenty or so digits blank): "Northeast Archives of Folklore and Oral History. Accession number 1197, tape 1197.1." The tape is copied (we use a fast-copy machine), the copy marked to correspond with the original (only with the designation "first generation" to distinguish it), and the copy tape used to calibrate the catalog or transcript every 100 digits (this also allows us to check the quality of the copy—things do foul up once in a while!). Then the original tape is placed in a sealed box and stored in a separate building from that housing the archives. Finally, the catalog or transcript is paginated, each page also receiving the accession number, and it is this page-and-accession number that is the basis for all indexing work (thus a reference to 1016.017 means that a particular item is to be found on page 17 in accession 1016).

Accessioning also includes cataloging and basic indexing work. A shelf card is prepared for each accession, indicating such basic data as interviewer, interviewee, place and date of interview, and general subjects covered. These cards are filed serially, and the same information is added to our cumulative catalog, which can be xeroxed on demand for any interested party. The general subject headings are then abstracted and placed in a card catalog subject file, while separate card files are also maintained for both interviewer and interviewee.

All of these operations are part of our basic procedure, and we try to keep them as up to date as possible. As time permits, we also maintain a personal and place-name file, which details every appearance of every name. Ultimately, we plan to have an equally detailed subject index, but that awaits development of a complete set of categories to fit our material—no small task. *Festina lente.*

People wishing to use our facilities for research fill out a form stating what they are looking for and what they plan to do with it. Then they sign a statement agreeing to publish nothing from Northeast Archives material without our written consent. Then we try to make them feel at home—the coffee pot is just down the hall.

At this point I would like to suggest that you arrange to deposit your tapes in more than one archives. If you are working independently— that is, not through any program or archives—you should consider depositing one copy of your tapes with the Archive of Folk Song in the Library of Congress (Washington, D.C. 20540) and another in a local, state, or regional repository. If you are working out of an established program or archives, they may already have such a duplicate deposit system. If they don't, it wouldn't be presumptuous of you to suggest that they look into the possibility of arranging for one. Don't, by the way, let the words "folk song" in the title put you off; the Archive of Folk Song is every bit as interested in straight oral history interviews as in old ballads. Their duplicating service is available either to you or to a cooperating archives. They will respect whatever reasonable restrictions on access and copying you may specify, and I am sure any cooperating local or regional archives will too.

There are two good reasons for making such duplicate deposits. First, it is a safety measure, since there is then almost no chance that fire or flood could wipe out your entire collection (except, of course, in the case of duplicate calamities!). Second, your primary data will be just that much more easily available, and, as we have already seen, that availability is less a convenience than it is an absolute requirement of good scholarship.

What about local, state, and regional archives and programs? How can you find out about them, assuming for the moment that you are not already associated with one? The Archive of Folk Song can supply you, for the asking, with a complete list of folklore and folk music archives in the United States and Canada, and I would also suggest that you write the American Folklife Center (Library of Congress, Washington, D.C. 20540) for information on any programs or activities they may know about in your area. In addition, although it is already somewhat out of date, the Oral History Association's directory, *Oral History in the United States* (1971, edited by Gary Shumway), listed in the Bibliography, is still very useful for finding the names and addresses of relevant programs. In Canada you should check with the Canadian Centre for Folk Culture Studies at the National Museum of Man, Ottawa, Ontario, and the Sound Archives of the Public Archives of Canada, 395 Wellington Street (also in Ottawa).

This brings me to my final bit of advice on this matter. When it comes to doing field work in folklore and oral history, don't make a fetish out of your independence. I know how easy that is to say and how hard it is to avoid. Most of us who use the techniques recommended in this manual are pursuing some special interest, and we tend to get very possessive of the territory our quest opens up to us, guarding it zealously against possible poachers, talking about "our" informants, and the like. I know that the idea of depositing my material in something other than an egg crate in my locked closet just didn't set right at first, but I allowed myself to be persuaded, and there have been no problems. I have always had all the control I felt I needed, and it has been a relief to know that all my work could not be wiped out by some freak accident. In short, I have never been sorry, and I all but guarantee that you won't be either.

On the Publication of Oral Materials

The tape-recording as a research document is still a comparatively new concept, and while forerunners of the technique can be found even as far back as the late nineteenth century, it has really been with us no more than thirty years.[14] Within those years, though, it has burgeoned, being used by many people for many different purposes, and has been subject to almost as many codes of conscience as there have been users and uses. As a result, when one picks up a book or article and reads something taken from a tape recording, he is seldom given any indication of its accuracy—that is, how close it is to the informant's actual words—and he is almost as seldom

14. The earliest published use of recorded materials is probably J. Walter Fewkes' "A Contribution to Passamaquoddy Folk-Lore," *Journal of American Folk-Lore* 3 (1890), pp. 257–280.

given any way to check that accuracy for himself. It is my contention that the reader must always be given both just as carefully as he would be given them for a quotation from a written or printed source.

But the problem is not quite as simple as it is for printed sources, where we have had both a long tradition of standard citation procedures and a strong tradition that insists on quotations accurate to the comma and letter. For the oral source, citation is not really much of a problem, since we can easily adapt the footnote and reference systems already used for printed sources. The real problem is accuracy, because, as we have already seen in our discussion of transcription, the question arises as to how accurate we intend or need to be. At the very least, an author owes his readers a clear and complete statement of his methods.

It should be assumed that the author is responsible for the transcriptions, either having made them himself or having checked existing transcriptions against the tape. If he is working from a transcript which he has not so checked, he should say so, and to the best of his ability he should describe what that transcript represents. If the transcript contains more than is on the tape—for instance, if it has been edited by the informant and includes his corrections and additions—the author should make that very clear. In addition to all this, the author should say what level of accuracy he has aimed at, what emendations he has made, and how such emendations are shown. Finally, he should indicate where the original tapes and transcripts are on deposit and how and under what circumstances they may be consulted (this should include a description of his system of citation). I offer the following as a model:

> All quotations preceded by an asterisk are taken verbatim from a tape recording; false starts, "uh's", and the like are the only material that has been eliminated without an indication of the omission by standard ellipsis marks. Within these verbatim passages, brackets indicate that the speaker's words were not absolutely clear, but this is my best guess as to what he was saying. In some places I have added words of my own to clarify a passage or to include a "stage direction." All such additions are both italicized and bracketed. Quotations not marked with an asterisk are taken as acccurately as possible from field notes, but I cannot guarantee word-for-word accuracy.
>
> The tapes and their accompanying transcripts are on file in the Northeast Archives of Folklore and Oral History, South Stevens Hall, Univer-

sity of Maine, Orono, Maine. Accession numbers (e.g. NA 423) are given in every case, and reference is given to page numbers in the catalog or transcript whenever possible (e.g. NA 423.157). Duplicate copies are on file in the Archive of Folk Song, in the Library of Congress, Washington, D.C.

The techniques given in the above model are ones that I have found very workable, and I impose them on all work, student and professional, coming out of the Northeast Archives. I have, by the way, found the technique of distinguishing taped from untaped quotations by marking the former with an asterisk very useful, since I have never yet written either a book or an article for which all the relevant data miraculously got recorded. But the exact techniques are less important than the recognition of the basic concept; that the reader has a right to know exactly what he is dealing with, and the author has an obligation to give him that information.

Appendix

A Compendium of Forms Used by the Northeast Archives of Folklore and Oral History

UNIVERSITY OF MAINE *at Orono*

Department of Anthropology
Northeast Archives of
Folklore and Oral History

Stevens Hall, South
Orono, Maine 04473
207/581-7466

July 31, 1973

Mr. John O'Connor
RFD # 2
Old Town, Maine

Dear Mr. O'Connor:

For many years the Argyle, Nebraska, and Pea Cove Booms played an important part in the social and economic life of this part of Maine, but they are swiftly becoming no more than a memory, and it won't be long before they are not even that. For things that were once so important, it is amazing how little information is available in libraries or anywhere else on just how boom work was done and what it was like to work on one. The Northeast Archives is therefore making a special effort to remedy this situation by talking to as many people as can be found who used to work on the booms.

A couple of days ago I was talking to Tom Burns up in Howland, who said that you had worked on Argyle Boom for many years and that if anyone could tell how the work went you could. Would you be willing to let me come around and talk to you about it? I am sure that you could add a great deal to our knowledge of boom operations, and I hope you'll agree to see me. I will be in touch with you in a couple of days. Meantime, thanks for any consideration you can give my request.

Sincerely yours,

Thurlow Blankenship
Research Assistant

Plate 2. This is the basic letter we used for making our first contact with possible informants for the Argyle Boom project. It is a reasonable model for any such letter.

NORTHEAST ARCHIVES OF FOLKLORE AND ORAL HISTORY
South Stevens Hall
University of Maine
Orono, Maine 04473

In consideration of the work the Northeast Archives
of Folklore and Oral History is doing to collect and preserve material of value for the study of ways of life past
and present in the New England-Maritimes area, I would
like to deposit with them for their use the items represented
by the accession number given below.

This tape or tapes and the accompanying transcript are
the result of one or more recorded, voluntary interviews
with me. Any reader should bear in mind that he is reading
a transcript of my spoken, not my written word and that the
tape, not the transcript, is the primary document.

It is understood that the Northeast Archives of Folklore and Oral History will, at the discretion of the
Director, allow qualified scholars to listen to the tapes
and read the transcript and use them in connection with their
research or for other educational purposes of a university.
It is further understood no copies of the tapes or transcript
will be made and nothing may be used from them in any
published form without the written permission of the
Director.

Signed: *Martin Callaghen*

Date: *July 11, 1978*

Understood and Agreed to:

Interviewer: *Thurlow Blackerdise*   Date: *July 11, 1978*

Director: _____   Date: _____

Accession number: _____

Plate 3. This is our standard release form, the one we use about 95 per cent
of the time. It gives the Archives the most discretion, which makes it the
most desirable from our point of view.

NORTHEAST ARCHIVES OF FOLKLORE AND ORAL HISTORY
South Stevens Hall
University of Maine
Orono, Maine 04473

In consideration of the work the Northeast Archives of
Folklore and Oral History is doing to collect and preserve
material of value for the study of ways of life past and
present in the New England-Maritimes area, I would like to
deposit with them for their use the items represented by the
accession number given below.

This tape or tapes and the accompanying transcripts are
the result of one or more recorded, voluntary interviews with
me. Any reader should bear in mind that he is reading a
transcript of my spoken, not written word and that the tape,
not the transcript, is the primary document.

It is understood that the Northeast Archives of Folklore
and Oral History will, at the discretion of the Director,
allow qualified scholars to listen to the tapes and read the
transcript and use them in connection with their research or
for other educational purposes of the university. It is
further understood that no copies of the tapes or transcript
will be made and nothing may be used from them in any published
form without my written permission, until _July 11, 1983_
after which time the Director's written permission will be
required.

Signed: _Martin Callaghen_

Date: _July 11, 1978_

Understood and Agreed to:

Interviewer:

Thurlow Blankenship   Date: _July 11, 1978_

Director:

_____   Date: _____

Accession Number_____

Plate 4. Release form B gives the Archives permission to let people listen to
the tapes and examine the catalogs or transcripts, but it leaves control over
publication and the making of copies with the informant.

C(7/20/73)

NORTHEAST ARCHIVES OF FOLKLORE AND ORAL HISTORY
South Stevens Hall
University of Maine
Orono, Maine   04473

In consideration of the work the Northeast Archives of
Folklore and Oral History is doing to collect and preserve
material of value for the study of ways of life past and present
in the New England-Maritimes area, I would like to deposit with
them for their use the items represented by the accession number
given below.

This tape or tapes and the accompanying transcripts are the
result of one or more recorded voluntary interviews with me.
Any reader of the transcript should bear in mind that he is
reading a transcript of my spoken, not my written, word, and that
the tape, not the transcript is the primary document.

I desire to place the following restrictions on this material.
That no use of any kind whatsoever is to be made of this

material until _____*July 11, 1983*_____.
After that time it is understood that the Northeast Archives of
Folklore and Oral History will, at the discretion of the Director,
allow qualified scholars to listen to the tapes and read the
transcripts in connection with their research or for other
educational purposes of a university. It is further understood
that after that time, no copies of any kind will be made of the
tape or transcript nor will anything be used from them in any
published form without the written permission of the Director.

Singed: *Martin Calloghan*

Date: *July 11, 1978*

Understood and agreed to:

Interviewer: *Hurlow Blankenship*   Date: *July 11, 1978*

Director: _____   Date: _____

Accession number: _____

Plate 5. Release form C is used when the informant wishes to "close" the
accession for some specific length of time. Until the given date, no one may
either listen to the tapes or examine the catalogs or transcripts thereof.

D(8/7/75)

NORTHEAST ARCHIVES OF FOLKLORE AND ORAL HISTORY
South Stevens Hall
University of Maine
Orono, Maine 04473

    This tape or tapes and the accompanying transcripts
are the result of one or more voluntary interviews held
by me with (name)___Martin Callaghan_____.
(address)_____Argyle, Maine_____.
Any reader of the transcript should bear in mind that he
is reading a transcript of our spoken, not our written,
words, and that the tape, not the transcript, is the primary document.

    Although he did not sign a formal release, it is my
understanding that the interviewee has no objections to
this material being used according to the terms of Form
__A__, a copy of which is attached to this form, with the
following exceptions:

Interviewer: _Thurlow Blankenship_

Date: _July 14, 1978_

Understood and agreed to:

Director: _____

Date: _____

Accession number:_____

Plate 6. Release form D is an entirely "self-serving" document which we
use when the informant expresses his willingness to have his material used
but refuses to sign anything. Naturally, we prefer not to use this form, but
occasionally it has been necessary.

NORTHEAST ARCHIVES OF FOLKLORE AND ORAL HISTORY
South Stevens Hall
University of Maine
Orono, Maine 04473

Interviewer Agreement

    I,   <u>Thurlow Blankenship</u>   , in view of the historical
       (Interviewer: type or print)
and scholarly value of the information contained in the inter-

view(s) with   <u>Martin Callaghan</u>
          (Interviewee(s): type or print)

and designated as accession number   <u>1243</u>   , knowingly and volun-
tarily permit the Northeast Archives of Folklore and Oral History
the full use of this information, the tapes and transcripts and
all other material in this accession, and hereby grant and assign
to the Northeast Archives of Folklore and Oral History all rights
of every kind pertaining to this information, whether or not such
rights are now known, recognized, or contemplated, except for such
restrictions as are specified below.

July 11, 1978
(Date)

                               Thurlow Blankenship
                              (Interviewer's signature)
Restrictions:

Understood and agreed to: _____
                                   (Director)

                                    _____
                                    (Date)

Plate 7. All interviewers sign one of these releases, usually after having
completed a series of interviews.

ACCESSION SHEET

Accession number: 1243

°Depositor: Thurlow Blankenship

°Permanent address: 172 No. Fourth St., Old Town, Me.

°Field Work Locations (state or province and town):   Argyle, Me.

°Description of Accession: A series of interviews with Martin Callaghan,
   89, in which he gives his life history, concentrating on his
   experiences as a woodsman, river-driver, and sawmill hand.

°Tapes (number):   12

°Photographs (number):   6   Photo Accession Numbers: 646-651

°Other material (specify):   a pair of spiked driving boots

Interviewer Agreement signed: 11/16/78

Release obtained: after each interview (last on 11/16/78). Form A

Special restrictions: none

°Catalog prepared: completed 11/24/78

Remarks:

ARCHIVES WORK

Shelf list card prepared: 12/1/78

Donor card prepared: 12/1/78

Tape copied: completed by 12/15/78

Transcription completed:

Pagination completed: 12/1/78

Indexing:

      Place names: 12/5/78   Personal names: 12/5/78

         Subject: preliminary 12/5/78

Plate 8. One of these forms is completed for each accession. The interviewer fills in all the blanks marked with an asterisk. The Archives fills in
the rest.

Interviewer's tape no.: 78.3   NAFOH Accession no.: 1243.2

Interviewer: Thurlow Blankenship   Address: 172 No. Fourth St., Old Town, Me.

Interviewee: Martin Callaghan   Address: Argyle, Me. (RFD # 2, Old Town,Me.)

Place of interview: MC's home   Date: July 11, 1978

Other people present: none

Equipment used: UHER 4000 Report L (NA TR-15)

Tape: Brand: 3M AV-176   Size reel: 5"   1 mil/1.5 mil   Speed: 1 7/8 ips

Cassette: Brand: C-30/C-60/C-120

Amount of tape used: (Side 1):   all   (Side 2):   1/3

Brief description of contents: a continuation of a series of life-history
    interviews, in which Mr. Callaghan tells of his winter lumbering
    on the Allagash, 1912-1913.

Index	TR-9 NAFOH	TR-15 Int.	Catalog
			(opening announcement)
	0015	0018	I never was away from home for more than a year--
			always back and forth. Went up to the Allagash.
			Went up to Axx Aroostook County potato picking once
			in the fall, I think in 1912 or 1913. It came a
			rainy spell and we were losing a lot of time, so
			we decided to go into the woods. We settled
			up with the man we were working for. Fred Dube
			of Winterville, this side of St. Francis before
			you come to Eagle Lake.
		0040	Ed Blackett and I went up to Fort Kent, and
			we ran into a fellow who was looking for men to
			go up the Allagash lumbering. We used to hang around
			a bar there in Claire, New Brunswick, just across
			the foot bridge from Fort Kent. This guy come
			in there, and we talked with him. He asked what

Plate 9. A sample of a complete catalog.

Index	NAFOH	Int.	Catalog
			we could do in the woods. I said almost anything, but I'd rather cook or drive a team. He said he had a young man to cook who'd done quite a bit of it, but if I came along and he couldn't handle it I could take over, and meanwhile I could drive team. So I drove team all winter there; the young fellow done xxxxghxx all right.
		0070	[At this point Callaghan's son dropped in for a visit, and the recorded was turned off for ten minutes or so]
			The man's name was Baptist Gilbear (?), and there were four or five brothers, all woods-men. The other brothers took charge in the woods for Condiff Lumber Co. I took a pair of horses, a green team, from Fort Kent, hitched them to a wagon and drove them up to where the Allagash comes into the St. John River. Pelkeys ran a farm there and sort of lodging house for people going back and forth.
		0090	Stayed there all night. They said we were going to take a boat in the morning. I was new to that country, so I didn't see how they were going to get a boat up there.
		0100	In the morning we hitched up a scow to some horses towing from the bank, big flat-bottomed scow 40-50 feet long, could take 25 ton of stuff. [phone rings;not his ring] and they didn't draw that much water. The horses could walk them

Plate 10. A sample of a complete catalog.

Northeast Archives of Folklore and Oral History

Accession 1243; Tape 1243.2

Interview with Martin Callaghan, Argyle, Maine

July 11,1978

Interviewer: Thurlow Blankenship

B: Blankenship

C: Callaghan

****

[Opening announcement]

B:When would you say you left home? (C:Well--) Or wasn't there
any one time or

C: No, the only time I -- I was always back and forth to home.
I never stayed away for over a year. I went away, I went up on
the Allagash. Let me see now. [pause 10 sec.] (0018) Yeah, I went
up to the Allagash -- I went up in Aroostook County ~~picking~~
potato picking time in the fall, another guy and I, and we
picked potatoes up there.

B: When would that have been ? Have you any idea?

C:When it was (B: Yeah) Well, I think that was nineteen-twelve
or thirteen, somewhere along there. I went up there to pick
potatoes, and we quit on the potatoes,⟨didn't like it⟩ stopped, and it come a
rainy spell, an awful rainy spell, and ~~s~~ we was losing a lot
of time picking potatoes, so I said "The hell with it. We might
just as well go somewhere into the woods." So we settled up
with him, old Fred Dube we was working for in Winterville.

B: He was working with you? (C: Eh?) Fred Dube, you say? (C: Yeah)
He was working with you?

C: No, for him. He was a farmer, and we was picking potatoes
for him. (B: Oh, I see.) in a place called Winterville, this side

Plate 11. A sample of a complete transcript.

of St Francis before you come to Eagle Lake. 0040 Anyway we quit
there and we went up to Fort Kent, the other guy and I.
B: Who was the fellow you went with?
C: Ed Blackett. We went up to Fort Kent, and we hung around
there a few days, and we ran into a fellow up there that was
going up the Allagash lumbering. He was looking for men. He was
just a young man, and we used to hang around a bar there was
there. In Fort Kent there was a foot bridge which went from Fort
Kent right across the river to Claire, New Brunswick, just a
                      foot
narrow bridge. And right at the end of that foot bridge was a
barroom. (B: On the Claire side?) On the Claire side. There was
a great big room there, had a bar there on one side of it where
                              used to hang around town, you know,
so we used to hang around there, and this guy come in there. (0057)
He was in from St. Francis. He was hiring men, wanted men to
go on up the Allagash. We talked with him, and he said,"You
fellows want to go up for me? What do you do in the woods?" Said
"I can do most anything I han Have to do." Says "I can cook and
I'm a teamster," I says, and I can do anything else, but I'd
rather cook or drive a team." So he says, "Well, I got a young
fellow wants to go up and cook, a young man, and he's supposed
to be quite a good cook. He worked at it quite a lot. He Wants
to go up and try it," he says, "but you go up and if he can't
handle it, why you can take over. But if he can handle it, you
can drive team."

    So we went up, and the young fellow done all right. (0070) So
I drove team. Worked there all winter. [At this point, Callaghan's
son dropped in for a visit, and the recorder was turned off for

Plate 12. A sample of a complete transcript.

ten <u>minutes</u> <u>or</u> <u>so</u>]

B: O.K. Here we go again. Now you were saying you just met this
guy in that barroom, and hired right there. Is that right?

C: Yup. His name was Baptist Gilbear (?), and there was four
of five brothers of them, and they was all woodsmen. The other
brothers took charge for the ~~smith~~ ^{Condiff} Lumber Company. That's who
I went up there for, the Condiff Lumber Company in Fort Kent.
So I took a pair of horses right there in Fort Kent, green team
they'd just ~~boughtxxx~~ brought in there. I took them and drove
them up the Allagash. We hooked them to a wagon and went up to
the mouth of the Allagash up where it come into the St. John's
River. There was a place there, kind of a lodging house, a big
farm, Pelkeys their name was, put up people going back and
forth, woodsmen. (0090) Anyway, we got there that night and we
stopped there all night. They said that we was going to take
the boat in the morning. Well, I was green to that country;
didn't know how they done business, and I see the mouth of
the river there was all just low water, rocks, and I says I don't
know what kind of a ~~i~~ place they're going to go with a boat here--
I said that to myself [chuckles]

In the morning we got up and went down, and that's the way
they towed it, in scows, _{with horses.} They were flat bottomed scows as long
as from here out to the road there. (B: That long? Maybe forty-
fifty feet?) Yeah, forty, fifty feet. They'd take twenty-five
tons of stuff on it, provisions and stuff. [<u>phone</u> <u>rings</u>, <u>not</u>
<u>his</u> <u>ring</u>] (B: It wouldn't draw much water.) Wouldn't draw much
water. She'd go anywheres in there on the river with that low

Plate 13. A sample of a complete transcript.

NORTHEAST ARCHIVES OF FOLKLORE AND ORAL HISTORY
SOUTH STEVENS HALL
UNIVERSITY OF MAINE
ORONO, MAINE 04473

REQUEST FOR USE OF ARCHIVES

Name: _J. ROBERT PIGOTT_   Date: _JULY 23, 1978_

Address: _54 COLLEGE AVENUE, CLINTON, NEW YORK_

Describe as completely as you can the sort of material or the
specific items you are looking for. If you are interested in a
particular town or other geographical area, be sure you mention
that too.

I AM LOOKING FOR INFORMATION ON HOW LOGGING
ROADS WERE MAINTAINED IN GOOD SHAPE THROUGHOUT THE
WINTER. I AM ESPECIALLY INTERESTED IN THE YEARS
BEFORE WORLD WAR I.

What use do you plan to make of this material? Are you writing a
book, article, dissertation? Are you a teacher who wants material
for lecture or classroom demonstration? Please be as specific as
possible.

THIS MATERIAL WILL BE USED FOR A CHAPTER IN A
BOOK I AM WRITING ON CHARLES MORRISSEY, ONE TIME
MAYOR OF GLENS FALLS, N.Y., AND A WELL-KNOWN PROHIBITIONIST
IN UPSTATE NEW YORK. IN HIS EARLY YEARS HE HAD
WORKED IN THE MAINE WOODS AS WHAT HE CALLED A
"ROAD MONKEY," WHICH HE DESCRIBED AS SOMEONE WHO
KEPT THE LOGGING ROADS OPEN.

I understand that all material is the property of Northeast
Archives of Folklore and Oral History and cannot be reproduced or
published in any form or way without the written permission of
the Director. I also agree to bear all costs of xeroxing, photographs, and tape publication in connection with my request.

Singed: _J. Robert Pigott_   Date: _JULY 23, 1978_

****

Disposition:

Plate 14. Anyone wishing to use the Archives completes and signs one of
these forms first.

A Brief Bibliography

This list is not exhaustive. It simply includes a few easily available items that I have found helpful. I have also tried to include items on oral history that most folklorists might not know about and a few general works on folklore for the benefit of oral historians. Many of these works have good bibliographies of their own, to which the reader can refer.

Agee, James, and Walker Evans. *Let Us Now Praise Famous Men.* New York: Ballantine Books, 1966 (first published 1939). Read it. That's enough said.

Baum, Willa K. *Oral History for the Local Historical Society.* Nashville: American Association for State and Local History, 1971. A very good introductory guide. Says a great deal in 62 pages. Bibliography.

_____. *Transcribing and Editing Oral History.* Nashville: American Association for State and Local History, 1977. Although written from the point of view of standard elitist oral history programs, this book is not narrowly doctrinaire. Contains a wealth of good advice. Includes a brief recording of an interview and that same interview transcribed. Has a good descriptive bibliography.

Brunvand, Jan Harold. *The Study of American Folklore: An Introduction.* 2d ed. New York: W.W. Norton, 1978. A good one-volume introductory folklore text, with individual chapters on the various genres, each of which is followed by an extremely useful and descriptive set of bibliographic notes. This is the book I always recommend to non-folklorists as an opener.

Colman, Gould P. "Oral History—An Appeal for More Systematic Procedures." *American Archivist* 28 (1965), pp. 79–83.

Curtiss, Richard D., Gary L. Shumway, and Shirley E. Stephenson, eds. *A Guide for Oral History Programs.* Fullerton: Oral History Program, California State University, 1973. Articles on various aspects of oral history by different well-known practitioners; a compendium of forms, guidelines, and procedures for the Fullerton program, one of the best-organized in the country; and a catalog of its holdings.

Dorson, Richard M. *American Folklore and the Historian.* Chicago: University of Chicago Press, 1971. Contains a series of essays by this leading American folklorist on the interrelationships of folklore and history, especially in such areas as traditional, folk, and oral history.

_____., ed. *Folklore and Folklife: An Introduction.* Chicago: University of Chicago Press, 1972. See entries below for List, MacDonald, and Roberts.

Goldstein, Kenneth S. *A Guide for Field Workers in Folklore.* Hatboro, Pa.: Folklore Associates, 1964 (also published as American Folklore Society Memoir 52). While this book seems to be written for the person planning a year's expedition to a foreign country, it is still a useful reference work for those of us who are not. Chapters on problem statement, pre-field preparation, establishing rapport, collecting methods, etc. Bibliography.

Gorden, Raymond L. *Interviewing: Strategy, Techniques, and Tactics.* Rev. ed. Homewood, Ill.: Dorsey Press, 1975. Very complete and readable. Covers much more than just tape-recorded interviews. Good on what makes an interview go well, what gets in the way, probes (especially good!), leading questions. Bibliography.

Langlois, William J. *A Guide to Aural History Research.* Victoria, B.C.: Aural History Programme, Provincial Archives of British Columbia, 1976. A procedures manual from a first-rate oral history program.

List, George. "Fieldwork: Recording Traditional Music." In Dorson, *Folklore and Folklife,* pp. 445–454. Selection of equipment, some tips on mike placement. Emphasizes the importance of good documentation. Bibliography.

MacDonald, Donald A. "Fieldwork: Collecting Oral Literature." In Dorson, *Folklore and Folklife,* pp. 407–430. Based largely on MacDonald's field work in Scotland. Emphasizes advance preparations, the recording of contexts, the use of tape recorders, tips for the beginner, directive and non-directive interviews, payment, etc. Very clear and useful. Bibliography.

Moss, William W. *Oral History Program Manual.* New York: Praeger, 1974. Based on the author's own experience in the John F. Kennedy Library's oral history program, this book is essential reading for anyone involved in large programs.

Notes and Queries on Anthropology. Sixth Edition. Revised and rewritten by a Committee of the Royal Anthropological Institution of Great Britain and Ireland. London: Routledge and Kegan Paul, 1951 (reprinted 1971). An extended guide to careful field observation and careful description. Intended especially for work with non-literate groups, but its usefulness is not limited to that. Covers all aspects of culture.

Oral History Review. 1973– . The annual publication of the Oral History Association, containing both regular articles on all aspects of oral history and selections from papers delivered at annual meetings. The proceedings of all earlier meetings are also available from OHA. For further information, write the Oral History Association, P.O. Box 13734, North Texas State University, Denton, Texas 76203.

O'Sullivan, Sean (O Suilleabhain, Sean). *A Handbook of Irish Folklore.* Dublin, 1942 (Reprinted Hatboro, Pa.: Folklore Associates, 1963). An exhaustive (699 pages) questionnaire covering almost every conceivable aspect of Irish folklore and folklife, and almost all of it is very easily adaptable to our own scene. A good place to turn if you want help in working up questions or in figuring out what to talk about in an interview.

Polunin, Ivan. "Stereophonic Magnetic Tape Recorders and the Collection of Ethnographic Field Data." *Current Anthropology* 6 (April, 1965), pp. 227–230. A method for recording the "event" on one track while making simultaneous observations on the other. Very clear text and diagrams.

_____. "Visual and Sound Recording Apparatus in Ethnographic Fieldwork." *Current Anthropology* 11 (February, 1970), pp. 3–22. A commentary with a reply by eight other scholars and a final rejoinder by the author. While the emphasis is on film and videotape techniques, there is enough here on tape recording to make it well worth checking. Bibliography.

Roberts, Warren E. "Fieldwork: Recording Material Culture." In Dorson, *Folklore and Folklife,* pp. 431–444. Contains excellent advice on how to document material objects such as buildings, tools, and the processes involved in various crafts. Bibliography.

Rosenberg, Neil V., ed. *Folklore and Oral History.* St. John's, Newfoundland: Memorial University of Newfoundland Folklore and Language Publication Series, Bibliographical and Special Series No. 3, 1978. Papers from the Second Annual Meeting of the Canadian Oral History Association, October 3–5, 1975. Twelve essays by scholars from various disciplines. The emphasis is on the Newfoundland scene, but the application is universal.

Shumway, Gary L. *Oral History in the United States: A Directory.* Denton, Texas: Oral History Association, 1971. Although out of date, it is still an extremely useful listing of some 230 projects from all over the United States. Projects are listed both by geographical area and by subject. Available from the Oral History Association, P.O. Box 13734, North Texas State University, Denton, Texas 76203.

Spradley, James P. and David W. McCurdy. *The Cultural Experience: Ethnography in Complex Society.* Chicago: Science Research Associates, 1972. "This book is based on the premise that the perspective of cultural anthropology is learned through ethnographic field work," say the authors, who then go on to give very readable and helpful advice on finding a "culture," discovering good informants and interviewing them, etc. Included are twelve student papers on everything from a car theft ring to firemen. A fine book. Bibliography.

Vansina, Jan. *Oral Tradition.* Chicago: Aldine, 1965. A pioneering work, based on the author's long acquaintance with African traditions of all kinds, in which he develops and discusses standards for evaluating the historicity of oral testimony. Essential reading.

Waserman, Manfred J. *Bibliography on Oral History.* Rev. ed. Denton,

Texas: Oral History Association, 1975. An annotated bibliography; very complete.

The following books are included as examples of four different ways tape-recorded interviews can be used in published works on folklore and folklife.

Degh, Linda. *People In The Tobacco Belt: Four Lives.* Ottawa: National Museum of Man, Mercury Series, Canadian Centre for Folk Culture Studies, Paper No. 13, 1975. The tape-recorded life histories of four Hungarian immigrants to Canada, with descriptive, interpretive, and analytical commentaries included for each one.

Ives, Edward D. *Argyle Boom.* Orono, Maine: *Northeast Folklore,* XVII, 1976. An important aspect of the lumber industry—the sorting and rafting of logs at the end of the drives—that ceased operation about 1930, described in detail by eighteen men who did the work. A very direct application of the methods and principles of documentation put forward by this manual.

Montell, William Lynwood. *The Saga of Coe Ridge: A Study in Oral History.* Knoxville: University of Tennessee Press, 1970. A good example of a local history in which the documentation is almost entirely oral folk testimony. The Preface is a good summary of the debate over the validity of such testimony.

Thornton, Ralph. *Me and Fannie: The Oral Autobiography of Ralph Thornton of Topsfield, Maine.* Orono, Maine: *Northeast Folklore,* XIV, 1973. A life history, selected and edited from many hours of tape recorded interview, as reorganized and edited both by the editor and the author himself.

Index